FRENCH COOKING ACADEMY

100 Essential Recipes
for the Home Cook

Stephane Nguyen
with Kate Blenkiron

Creators of
French Cooking Academy

PAGE STREET
PUBLISHING CO.

PAGE STREET
PUBLISHING CO.

First published in 2023 by
Page Street Publishing Co.
27 Congress Street, Suite 1511
Salem, MA 01970
www.pagestreetpublishing.com

Distributed by Macmillan, sales in Canada by The Canadian Manda Group.

26   25   24   23   1   2   3   4   5

ISBN-13: 978-1-64567-979-0
ISBN-10: 1-64567-979-9

Library of Congress Control Number: 2022947665

Cover and book design by Rosie Stewart for Page Street Publishing Co.
Photography by Kate Blenkiron
Cover styling by Jo O'Keefe

Printed and bound in China

Dedicated to my mother, Catherine,
who would have been proud of this book.

Contents

Introduction 6

Tips to Improve Your Cooking 8

PART 1: FRENCH STAPLES 11

White Chicken Stock 12

Brown Chicken Stock 13

Homestyle Demi-Glace 15

Quick Seafood Stock 16

Classic French Dressings 17

Steak Herb Butter 21

Homemade Mayonnaise 22

Classic Béchamel 23

Easy Béarnaise 24

No-Fuss Hollandaise 26

Chicken Velouté Sauce 27

Garden-Fresh Tomato Sauce 29

Morel Mushroom Sauce with Madeira Wine 30

Burgundy-Style Red Wine Sauce 32

Mascarpone Whipped Cream 33

Traditional French Meringue 35

Crêpes 36

All-Purpose Short Crust 39

Pastry Cream 40

Choux Pastry 43

PART 2: TO START 45

Small Bites for All Occasions 45

Tapenade 47

Eggs Mimosa 48

Baked Eggs with Tomato, Capers and Croutons 51

Greek-Style Mushrooms 52

Gougères 55

Tomato and Mustard Feuilleté 56

Caramelized Onion and Bacon Quiche 59

Grand Aioli Platter 60

Timeless Salads, Soups and Appetizers 63

Lyonnaise Bistro Salad 65

Farmhouse Lentil Salad 66

Warm Goat Cheese Salad 69

Classic Parisian Salad 70

Niçoise Salad 73

Cucumbers in Cream Dressing 74

Parisian Carrot Salad 77

Spring Leeks with Vinaigrette 78

Celeriac Salad with Homemade Mayonnaise 81

Asparagus with Mousseline Sauce 82

French Onion Soup with Port Wine 85

Crécy Carrot Soup 86

Creamy Corn Velouté 89

My Signature Chicken Soup 90

Classic Salmon Tartare 93

Baked Eggs à la Florentine 94

Mackerel Escabèche 97

Creamy Ham and Cheese Feuilleté 98

Twice-Baked Cheese and Ham Soufflé with Gourmet Mushrooms 100

PART 3: EXQUISITE MAINS, SEAFOOD AND SIDES 103

Mouthwatering Meats and Poultry 103

Market Rotisserie Chicken with Potato and Tomato Garnish 104

Bistro Steak and Fries with Herb Butter 107

Maître d' Steak Tartare 108

Seared Chicken Breasts in Creamy Mushroom Sauce 111

Beef Daube with Spring Carrots 112

Normandy-Style Pork Chops with Cider and Calvados Sauce 115

Steak au Poivre 116

Chicken Chasseur 119

Braised Lamb Shanks in Port Wine 120

Braised Chicken in Tarragon Sauce 123

Panfried Steak with Red Wine
Sauce   124

Beaujolais-Style Chicken   127

Baked Lamb Chops
"Champvallon" with Onions
and Potatoes   128

Pork Chops with Mustard and
Gherkin Sauce   130

Slow-Cooked Beef in Dark
Belgian Beer   133

Braised Chicken the
Corsican Way   134

Red Wine Beef Ragout
Dauphinoise   137

Poulet Sauté Alice   138

Creamy Sautéed Chicken with
Cider and Calvados   141

Dishes from the Sea   143

Marinière Mussels with
Pommes Frites   145

Breaded Fish Filets with
Tartare Sauce   146

Poached Fish in Tomato and
Vermouth Sauce   149

Bistro Fish Filets with Sautéed
Potatoes   150

Fish and Scallops à la
Mornay   153

Fish with Saffron
Velouté Sauce   154

Oven-Baked Fish with White
Vermouth *à la Minute*   157

**Classic and Regional
Sides   159**

French-Style Pilaf Rice   161

Lyonnaise Sautéed
Green Beans   162

Classic Cauliflower Gratin   165

Sautéed Potatoes in
Duck Fat   166

Potato Gratin with
Mushrooms   169

Duchess Potatoes   170

Potatoes Boulangère   173

Brittany White Beans   174

Basque-Style Sautéed
Courgettes   177

French Garden Peas
with a Twist   178

**PART 4: TREATS, TARTS
AND DESSERTS TO PLEASE
EVERYONE   181**

Baked Coconut Treats   183

Old-Fashioned Macarons   184

Vanilla Rice Pudding with
Raisins and Grand Marnier   187

Commercy-Style
Madeleines   188

Family-Size Crème
Caramel   191

Classic Flambéed Crêpes   192

Artisan Crustless
Cheesecake   195

Easy Chocolate Fondant   196

Normandy Apple Tart with
Calvados   199

Choux Nuts   200

Choux Chantilly   203

Parisian Custard Tart   204

Petit Raspberry
Mille-Feuille   207

Traditional Basque Cake with
Black Cherry Jam   208

Almond Cream Pithivier   210

Mère Brazier's Floating Island
Dessert   213

Ice Cream and Meringue
Vacherin with Berries   215

Acknowledgments   218

About Us   219

Index   220

INTRODUCTION

If you're feeling a bit intimidated about diving into the world of authentic French cuisine, let me tell you—I've been there too. Several years ago, as a Frenchman starting a new life abroad, I was craving the tastes of home and realized the only way to satisfy my gastronomic desires was to learn how to cook like a French pro. The problem? I had limited experience in the kitchen, and the thought of recreating classic dishes seemed impossible.

But, being a curious person, I wondered if I could teach myself French cooking simply by following culinary texts. And so began my epic journey from IT guy to French cooking teacher. I spent the first years sharing videos online demonstrating the techniques I was learning from culinary institute textbooks and old, forgotten cookbooks (some dating back centuries!). As I continued to hone my skills, I discovered the famous *Le Guide Culinaire* by Auguste Escoffier, and let me tell you—it was a game changer. Escoffier's philosophy of sharing culinary knowledge resonated deeply with me and inspired me to start the French Cooking Academy online cooking school with my Australian wife, Kate. Now, we're on a mission to help foodies all over the world fast-track their French cooking journey and master the art of French cuisine.

So, for our first cookbook, I'm sharing the essential things that took my own cooking to new heights and that are most useful for home cooking. We've set out to create a book that anyone can use regardless of cooking experience, with accessible recipes broken down into a classic bistro-style menu. Not only are the recipes home cooking–friendly, but they're also crafted with the aim of learning by doing. So, the more recipes you make, the more your skills and confidence will grow. While there are a handful of more-involved recipes for those up for the challenge, most of the recipes in this book are suitable for beginners. No kitchen jargon, complex explanations or lengthy lists of hard-to-source ingredients. These recipes are easily made using ingredients found in your local supermarket or specialty store (for better-quality produce). For the rest, your home kitchen should have all the things you need. This book is all about showcasing that French cooking doesn't have to be complex, and you don't need to spend hours in the kitchen to prepare impressive meals for your favorite people. But don't mistake easy for bland. A simple recipe with the right techniques and combination of ingredients can be a palatable wonder, pleasing the pickiest of guests. Suffice to say, the recipes here have all passed the taste test.

While we couldn't resist including such classics as the Parisian Custard Tart (page 204), Chicken Chasseur (page 119) and Niçoise Salad (page 73), a parade of French cooking clichés is not the focus here. Instead, you'll find recipes that have stood the test of time and dishes that have graced every kind of French table, from kings to peasants and fine restaurants to the humble home. This is a cooking journey faithful to French gastronomy, our way of life and customs.

Learn how to poach a fish and make a delicious sauce in 30 minutes; bring unique tastes to dishes by cooking with beer, wine and spirits; master the art of pan sauces; get a taste of regional one-pot recipes with Beaujolais-Style Chicken (page 127) and Slow-Cooked Beef in Dark Belgian Beer (page 133); take your taste buds to Corsica with the Braised Chicken the Corsican Way (page 134); or walk in the footsteps of the first female Michelin-starred chef, Mère Brazier, by re-creating her famous Floating Island Dessert (page 213). Every recipe in this book has a story to tell or something to teach.

We hope you enjoy our first book and try as many recipes as you can. All you need is a good appetite and your favorite people to share the culinary experience with. And provided you don't have anything against cream and butter, you're in for a deliciously good time.

Bon appétit!

Stephane Nguyen

- **Mise en place, people!** *Mise en place* is a French culinary term that means "putting in place" or "everything in its place." In layman's terms, it's the preparation of everything you need before you start to cook. Although the term is more often associated with commercial kitchens, measuring, preparing ingredients and organizing cookware before you start cooking is half the job done. In this book, most recipes start with a mise en place instruction to prompt you on important preparations you need to make ahead, oven settings and specialty cookware you may need. Although it may feel odd at first, you'll quickly fall into the habit of taking a moment to prepare your mise en place rather than diving headfirst into the recipe directions. You may even derive a sense of pride and accomplishment from the practice, like a true chef.

- **Good cooking starts with good ingredients.** Search for the freshest ingredients you can find. Cooking is like most things in life: What you put in is what you get out. Choose fresh, seasonal and locally grown food where you can. Better still, grow your own if there is room. For us, this means growing our own vegetables, cooking with the seasons and seeking out produce from local farmers and producers. Starting with "fresh" makes a huge difference to the taste of your dishes.

- **Take butter (and cream) seriously.** Yes, we love our butter in France. As Julia Child famously said, "With enough butter, anything is good." So, if you want the best possible results in French cooking, try to use good quality butter. The fat content needs to be at least 82 percent for a rich and creamy taste. Anything below that is not considered real butter in France. As for the cream, where possible, try to get your hands on an organic product that does not contain thickeners or gelatin. Trust me, these little details go a long way in French cooking.

- **Oven settings used in this book.** All oven temperatures are for fan-forced ovens unless stated otherwise.

- **Control oven temperatures.** Regardless of the model you use, placing a small oven thermometer inside the oven is a great way to ensure that you're cooking and baking at the correct temperature for a recipe. Unfortunately, consumer-grade ovens are not always precise and can be off by up to 15 to 25°F (10 to 15°C). Often, the wrong temperature can be the difference between culinary success and failure.

- **Measurements.** For our international audience, we've listed imperial measurements followed by their metric equivalents slightly rounded so that ingredients can be easily measured using scales, measuring cups and spoons at home. Where quantities need to be precise for a successful result (very important for baking!), ounces and fluid ounces are used for imperial measurements. I also recommend getting your hands on a digital scale to help with measuring ingredients accurately.

- **Toasting flour.** Toasting the flour for sauces and ragouts removes that raw floury taste and adds a pleasant nutty aroma. To make toasted flour, place a few tablespoons (about 15 g) of all-purpose flour in a small saucepan over high heat and stir constantly until the flour turns a chestnut color and starts to smell nutty. Make in batches and store in an airtight container to have at the ready for any savory recipe that calls for a sprinkle of flour over the ingredients.

- **Don't overdo the salt.** When it comes to using salt in French cooking, the rule of thumb is to season meats and fish just before cooking or when stated in the recipe, and then round out with seasoning to taste at the end. Keep in mind that as ingredients cook, natural salts are released, and by the time the dish is ready and cooking liquids have reduced, the overall saltiness will have increased. By adding too much salt during cooking, you run the risk of oversalting the dish. Remember, you can always add salt, but you can't remove it.

- **Don't let the food get cold.** Keeping and serving food warm in a restaurant is paramount, and it should be the same at home. Place your serving dishes and plates in a warm oven to ensure the dish is deliciously warm when it hits the table.

- **The wow factor of a homemade stock:** Behind every good sauce and stew is a great stock. Homemade stocks and demi-glace are the pillars of French cooking used to create deep, rich flavors in many dishes. They're like the chorus line in soups, sauces and ragouts in that, while not the star of the show, they work hard in the background to greatly enhance the overall flavor. Making your own stock brings a superior result compared to a premade product and will set your cooking apart.

- **Make your stock in large batches** and store in the fridge for up to 48 hours or in the freezer for up to 3 months. When using a frozen stock, always sterilize it first by bringing it briefly to a boil.

- **A tip for bakers.** Never throw away unused egg whites. Rather, keep them in an airtight container in the fridge for several weeks or freeze for several months. They're useful for anything baking, especially meringues.

- **Making vanilla sugar.** An easy way to make vanilla sugar is to keep fresh vanilla beans in a jar filled with granulated sugar. Not only do they keep, but they will also infuse your sugar with a lovely vanilla flavor. You can also recycle leftover vanilla beans by rinsing and drying them and popping them back in the sugar jar.

- **Above all else, enjoy!** When it comes to home cooking, there's one thing you need to remember—mistakes happen. But don't let a burnt dish or a messy kitchen get you down. At the end of the day, cooking is all about bringing together your favorite people to enjoy a delicious meal and each other's company. Or, if you're cooking solo, it's about taking a moment to unwind and savor the flavors of your hard work. So, don't stress about the appearance of your dish—as long as it tastes amazing, that's all that matters. Embrace the cooking experience with a curious mindset and a positive attitude, and why not pour yourself a glass of wine while you're at it? Remember, the true goal of cooking is to create memories and moments that will last a lifetime. So, grab your apron and let's get cooking!

Part 1: French Staples

As a self-taught cook, I can say from experience that learning the art of French cooking is much easier than the myth of its complexity would have you believe. Once you master a handful of basic techniques, your confidence in the kitchen will grow, and you'll be surprised by how quickly your cooking skills expand. The staples here represent essential culinary techniques you'll find in many French recipes, sweet and savory. We've done our best to focus on what matters for the home cook, with skills you can use on repeat to build dishes and variations, so that one recipe becomes many. You will learn how to make sauces and stocks and the simple baking techniques that will catapult your French dishes into wow territory. This section also serves as a handy reference guide for when a recipe in this book calls for a particular staple method, which gives you the opportunity to experience their true usefulness (and deliciousness) in the kitchen.

WHITE CHICKEN STOCK

White chicken stock is a great recipe for beginners. This version is easy to make and only requires chicken wings, vegetables and aromatics. The resulting stock is perfect for soups and white sauces, and it can also be used to cook rice, risotto and vegetables for added flavor. Remember to use high-quality ingredients for the best taste, and you'll never want to use store-bought stock again.

Makes 2½ cups (600 ml)

1 lb (500 g) chicken wings or chicken carcass (or a combination of both)
5 cups (1.2 L) cold water
2 whole cloves
½ onion
½ carrot, roughly chopped
½ leek (white part only), roughly chopped
¼ celery rib, roughly chopped
1 clove garlic, bruised
1 small bay leaf
1 sprig thyme
Pinch of coarse salt
5 whole peppercorns

MISE EN PLACE

Chop the chicken into three or four pieces and place in a bowl. Rinse under cold water until the water in the bowl becomes clear, then drain and pat dry.

Place the chicken in a stockpot and fill the pot with the water. Bring to a light boil and remove the foam on the surface before adjusting the heat to low. Add the cloves, onion, carrot, leek, celery, garlic, bay leaf, thyme, salt and peppercorns to the pot and simmer uncovered for 2 hours, occasionally skimming off any foam that floats to the surface (the cleaner the stock, the better the result).

Remove the stock from the heat, and let it rest for 15 minutes before straining the liquid through a fine-mesh sieve into a large bowl or jar. Allow the stock to cool to room temperature before using it.

TIP

Don't let the cooked chicken wings go to waste. Strip the meat off each piece, and use the shreds in pasta or as a garnish for quiche. I love using the shredded chicken to make chicken sandwiches with lettuce, tomatoes and Homemade Mayonnaise (page 22).

BROWN CHICKEN STOCK

This recipe will teach you how to create a rich and flavorful brown chicken stock from scratch. By using roasted chicken wings and carcass, you will be able to achieve a deep amber color and a distinct roasted chicken taste that will take your sauces and stews to the next level. Even if you're new to stock making, don't be intimidated. The process is simple, and the result is really worth it.

Makes 8½ cups (2 L)

3 lb (1½ kg) chicken wings or chicken carcass (or a combination of both)

2 carrots, roughly diced

1 onion, roughly diced

¼ celery rib, sliced

½ cup (120 ml) boiling water + 85 fl oz (2.5 L) water, divided

3 button mushrooms, quartered

1 bay leaf

1 sprig fresh thyme

1 clove garlic, halved

½ tsp coarse salt

5 whole peppercorns

MISE EN PLACE

Preheat the oven to 450°F (230°C). Use a cleaver or a large knife to cut each chicken piece into four or more pieces.

Roast the chicken pieces in a large roasting pan for 20 to 30 minutes until dark brown.

Add the carrots, onion and celery, mixing them with the chicken, and roast for 5 minutes, or until the vegetables become light brown and crispy.

Remove from the oven and scrape the chicken and vegetables into a stockpot. Pour the ½ cup (120 ml) of boiling water into the roasting pan, and use a wooden spoon to detach the caramelized juices before adding this liquid to the stockpot. Now, add the 85 fluid ounces (2½ L) of water and bring to a light boil.

Add the mushrooms, bay leaf, thyme, garlic, salt and peppercorns. Remove the foam floating on the surface of the stock, and simmer, uncovered, for 2 hours, occasionally scooping any foam off the surface. Remove the stock from the heat and let it cool for 15 minutes before carefully straining it through a fine-mesh sieve into a large bowl. Cover the stock and refrigerate it for a few hours, or overnight, until the fat solidifies on the surface. Once the fat has solidified, it can be easily scooped off before using the stock.

HOMESTYLE DEMI-GLACE

When it comes to making a mouthwatering sauce, the use of a demi-glace is a valuable shortcut that will save you a few hours in the kitchen. Used as a sauce base, a demi-glace is stock that is enhanced with meat trimmings, aromatics and a splash of wine, and thickened with a touch of flour. The method here allows you to start with a good-quality premade bone broth or stock and transform it into a versatile sauce base that can be used in many recipes in this book. If you want to go "pro," use the Brown Chicken Stock (page 13).

Makes 1¼ cups (300 ml)

2 cups (500 ml) good-quality premade veal or chicken stock or bone broth (without salt or salt-reduced)

1 lb (500 g) chicken carcass or a combination of carcass and wings

1 tbsp (15 ml) cooking oil

½ carrot, diced

½ onion, diced

¼ celery rib, sliced

1 clove garlic, halved

2 small button mushrooms, quartered

2 tsp (10 g) tomato paste

1 sprig thyme

1 bay leaf

⅓ cup (80 ml) full-bodied red wine or dry white wine

1 tbsp (8 g) toasted flour (page 9)

¼ tsp salt

1 tsp peppercorns

MISE EN PLACE

Bring the stock to a light boil and set aside. Roughly chop the chicken carcass and/or wings. Toast the flour according to page 9.

In a stockpot or large heavy-bottomed saucepan, heat the oil over medium-high heat and sear the chicken pieces for 10 to 12 minutes, or until the meat is a deep brown but not burnt. Scoop out the meat pieces and set aside. Remove any excess fat from the pot.

Lower the heat to medium, and add in the carrot, onion, celery, garlic and mushrooms, and cook for 2 minutes. Add the tomato paste, thyme and bay leaf and stir well. Pour in the wine and deglaze by scraping the bottom of the pot with a wooden spoon to detach and blend the caramelized juices into the liquid. Reduce until roughly 2 tablespoons (30 ml) of liquid remain.

Return the chicken pieces to the pot and stir in the toasted flour before pouring in the stock and adding the salt and peppercorns. Wait for the liquid to come to a boil, then simmer for 30 minutes to reduce the liquid by roughly half, occasionally removing any foam that forms on the surface.

Remove the pot from the heat and let the demi-glace cool for 15 minutes before straining it through a fine-mesh sieve into a bowl. The demi-glace can be used immediately, kept in the fridge for 3 days or frozen for several months.

TIP
When using the demi-glace to make certain sauces, the wine can be replaced with red port or Madeira wine.

QUICK SEAFOOD STOCK

Nowadays, sourcing fish bones to make a fish stock at home is not an easy task, and there's little choice but to resort to flavorless premade stuff that often tastes like a mussel that has been stewed in a pot of water. Fortunately, there's a quick and easy alternative that delivers the full flavor needed to whip up a range of fish and seafood dishes. For this recipe, I start with a store-bought fish stock and transform it into a tasty, all-purpose seafood stock by using fresh clams.

Makes 1 cup (250 ml)

10.5 oz (300 g) fresh or frozen clams

1¼ cups (300 ml) premade fish stock

1 tbsp (15 g) unsalted butter

1 tbsp (10 g) finely diced shallot

1 tbsp (15 g) finely sliced leek (white part only)

1 button mushroom, finely sliced

1 tsp finely chopped fresh parsley

1 tbsp (15 ml) white wine

Pinch of salt

MISE EN PLACE

If using fresh clams, rinse and clean thoroughly.

Bring the stock to a light boil and set aside.

In a medium-sized saucepan, melt the butter over low heat, and then gently cook the shallot, leek and mushroom for just a few minutes to avoid coloration. Add the clams, parsley and wine, pop on the lid and increase the heat to high. Cook for 3 minutes, or until the clams open. Pour in the stock, add the salt and bring to a boil. Then, simmer for 15 minutes to concentrate the flavors.

Strain the stock through a fine-mesh sieve into a bowl, leaving 1 tablespoon (15 ml) of liquid in the pan. (This section of the stock usually contains sand and hard residue, and you don't want this floating around in your beautiful stock.) Filter a second time, this time using a cheesecloth-lined sieve to guarantee a grit-free stock. Once filtered, use immediately or keep refrigerated for a few days. I don't advise freezing it because this stock tastes best fresh.

CLASSIC FRENCH DRESSINGS

Vinaigrette, commonly known around the world as French dressing, is essentially an emulsion of oil and vinegar with seasoning. The French have been using vinaigrette since the 15th century to season salads, vegetables and meat dishes. Hundreds of variants have evolved over time, and I couldn't possibly list them all here, but I can share a handful of all-time classics along with some lesser-known versions that I find particularly tasty.

THE BASE ELEMENTS

Vinegar: The quality of vinegar can make or break a dressing. I tend to favor red or white wine vinegar varieties, but cider vinegar or sherry (Jerez) vinegar are great too. It's also interesting to try fruity varieties, such as raspberry vinegar. Avoid distilled white vinegar at all costs.

Oil: It pays to play around with different oils to vary the flavor. Sunflower, peanut, grapeseed, canola and olive oil are all good but mainstream. For a more distinctive flavor, try walnut, avocado or even macadamia oil.

Herbs: Always go fresh and chop your herbs finely. Experiment with tarragon, chervil, parsley, chives, basil, shallots or garlic.

Mustard: Mustard used in a vinaigrette is typically a strong Dijon, but you can use whole-grain mustard too.

THE CLASSICS
Traditional Vinaigrette

Pinch of salt

Pinch of freshly ground pepper

1 tbsp (15 ml) vinegar

3 tbsp (45 ml) oil

Mustard Vinaigrette

Pinch of salt

Pinch of freshly ground pepper

1 tbsp (15 ml) white wine vinegar or cider vinegar

1 tsp strong Dijon mustard

3 tbsp (45 ml) sunflower oil

Fresh Herb Vinaigrette

Pinch of salt

Pinch of freshly ground pepper

1 tbsp (15 ml) white or red wine vinegar

1 tsp strong Dijon mustard

3 tbsp (45 ml) sunflower oil

1 tbsp (3 g) chopped fresh mixed herbs of your choice (you can also add some thin slices of shallots or a pinch of chopped garlic)

REGIONAL VINAIGRETTES
Burgundy-Style Vinaigrette

Pinch of salt

Pinch of freshly ground pepper

1 tbsp (15 ml) red wine vinegar

¼ tsp Dijon mustard

3 tbsp (45 ml) walnut oil

Lemon and Rosemary Vinaigrette

Pinch of salt

Pinch of freshly ground pcpper

2 tbsp (30 ml) fresh lemon juice

½ tsp honey (optional)

3 tbsp (45 ml) olive oil

Pinch of finely chopped fresh rosemary

(continued)

SPECIALTY VINAIGRETTES

These vinaigrettes marry beautifully with lettuce varieties that have robust leaves with a crunch, such as radicchio, chicory, romaine and frisée (endive).

Creamy Garlic Vinaigrette

Pinch of salt

Pinch of freshly ground pepper

1 tsp white wine vinegar

½ tsp Dijon mustard

1 clove garlic, pressed with a garlic press

1 tbsp (15 ml) olive oil

2 tbsp (30 ml) heavy cream

Roquefort (Blue Cheese) Vinaigrette

2 pinches of freshly ground pepper

1 tbsp (15 ml) red wine vinegar

1.5 oz (40 g) Roquefort cheese, flattened with a fork

5 tbsp (75 ml) heavy cream

1 tbsp (5 g) finely chopped fresh chives

The method for making a vinaigrette is always the same. In a small bowl, start with the salt and pepper, followed by the vinegar and mustard (if using). Mix together until the salt dissolves before adding the oil and any other listed ingredients. Always finish a vinaigrette with a vigorous stir to create the emulsion. These vinaigrette recipes can be used to jazz up a range of dishes from salads to appetizers and sides to mains.

TIP

Perhaps this is something your mother never told you, but avoid drinking wine with a salad dressed with a vinaigrette. The vinegar in the dressing will kill the taste of the wine.

STEAK HERB BUTTER

If you love steak and have traveled to France, you may have heard of the famous entrecôte butter sauce. This sumptuous sauce was invented in the 1930s at the famous Genevese brasserie Café de Paris by Mr. Boubier and was regarded as one of best butter sauces on the planet. The original recipe remains a closely guarded secret, but whispers among French chefs have inspired this recipe, which is packed with tangy and sharp flavors. Although this herb butter can be kept in the freezer, it tastes best when consumed within a few days after it's been made.

Makes 4 servings

¾ cup (170 g) unsalted butter

1 tbsp (15 ml) ketchup

1 tsp Dijon mustard

1 tbsp (10 g) finely diced shallot

2 anchovy filets (from a jar), finely chopped

4 tsp (6 g) finely chopped fresh tarragon

2 tbsp (6 g) finely chopped fresh parsley

½ clove garlic, crushed with a garlic press

1 tsp cognac

1 tsp white vermouth

1 tsp Worcestershire sauce

Few drops of Tabasco®

½ tsp salt

Pinch of ground white pepper

½ tsp sweet paprika

½ tsp curry powder

1 tsp dried herbes de Provence or Italian seasoning

MISE EN PLACE

Let the butter sit at room temperature until soft enough to spread flat effortlessly with the back of a spoon.

In a small bowl, combine the ketchup, mustard, shallot, anchovies, tarragon, parsley, garlic, cognac, vermouth, Worcestershire sauce, Tabasco, salt, pepper, sweet paprika, curry powder and herbes de Provence and stir well. Let this aromatic flavoring macerate at room temperature for 15 minutes.

In a separate bowl, use a spatula to work the butter into a paste. Slowly incorporate the aromatic flavoring into the butter a little at a time, stirring gently, until the ingredients are well distributed. Spoon the butter into a log shape on a piece of plastic wrap and roll, sealing the plastic tight at both ends. Chill the butter in the fridge for at least 2 hours, but overnight is best to allow the flavors to infuse. Use sliced over steak, fish or vegetables.

HOMEMADE MAYONNAISE

Knowing how to whip up a mayonnaise whenever a recipe calls for it is an indispensable skill to have in French cooking. It only takes 10 minutes and is so much creamier and more flavorful than anything you can buy at the store. To get a great taste and consistency every time, always ensure the ingredients are at room temperature and use precise measurements for the oil and seasoning. Do this and you'll never want to buy the store-bought stuff again.

Makes about ¾ cup (185 g) mayonnaise

2 pinches of salt

Pinch of ground white pepper

1 large egg yolk, at room temperature

1 tsp Dijon mustard

½ cup (120 ml) grapeseed or sunflower oil, divided

2 tsp (10 ml) white wine vinegar or fresh lemon juice

MISE EN PLACE

Make sure all the ingredients are at room temperature before you start.

In a large glass bowl set on a folded tea towel, combine the salt, pepper, egg yolk and mustard. Whisk together for 1 minute. Add 1 tablespoon (15 ml) of the oil and whisk vigorously until it is fully incorporated with the egg mixture. Repeat this step two more times.

At this stage, the mixture should start to resemble a mayonnaise but will still be a little liquid. You can start adding the oil in larger quantities, between 2 and 3 tablespoons (30 and 45 ml) at a time while whisking constantly. As you add more oil, the mayonnaise will become stiff, and whisking will become harder, which is normal. Just keep going until all the oil is added.

Once you have a firm, billowy, yellow mayonnaise, whisk in the vinegar to add a little zing and create a paler color. Resist the temptation to overdo the vinegar, as too much will make the mayonnaise runny. Mayonnaise tastes best served chilled, so keep in the fridge covered for at least 30 minutes before serving. Store for up to 24 hours in the fridge.

TIP

Always use a large glass bowl and a balloon whisk. You need plenty of space to lend a little vigor to your whisking and incorporate air into the mayonnaise.

VARIATIONS

Try these variations by adding the ingredients after the mayonnaise is done:

Sweet piquillo mayonnaise with cold chicken, eggs or fish: Add 1 teaspoon of tomato coulis (page 29), 3 tablespoons (35 g) of finely chopped roasted piquillo pepper and a pinch of cayenne pepper.

Alternatively, make a fiery harissa mayonnaise to add some spice to steak sandwiches and hamburgers: Add 2 teaspoons (10 g) of harissa paste and 2 teaspoons (5 g) of sweet paprika.

CLASSIC BÉCHAMEL

If there's one sauce you should master at home, it's béchamel. The list of things you can do with this silky white sauce is almost endless. There's an art to making a good béchamel; a poor recipe can lead to a tasteless, thick paste that you could plaster a wall with. This recipe produces a smooth, all-purpose béchamel that can be used in a wide range of tasty applications. Use for vegetables, pasta bakes or as a base to make sauces, or spread it on top of a toasted sandwich (croque monsieur, anyone?).

Makes 2 scant cups (450 ml) of sauce

1 oz (30 g) unsalted butter
1 oz (30 g) all-purpose flour
2 cups (500 ml) whole milk
2 whole cloves
½ onion
1 bay leaf
1 sprig thyme
1 tsp salt
2 pinches of ground white pepper
Pinch of freshly grated nutmeg

In a medium-sized saucepan, melt the butter over low heat, and then add the flour all at once. To make a roux, stir with a wooden spoon until the flour and butter combine to form a paste. Cook for 2 minutes, then immediately remove from the heat, setting aside to cool.

Meanwhile, in another medium-sized saucepan, combine the milk, cloves, onion, bay leaf, thyme, salt, pepper and nutmeg. Slowly bring to a light boil, stirring from time to time.

As soon as the milk is warm, strain half of it over the cold roux sitting in the other saucepan and use a whisk to fully blend with the roux before adding the rest of the milk. Bring the sauce to a boil over medium heat while stirring constantly. (Bringing it gradually to a boil is the key to a smooth sauce, so don't be hasty.)

When the sauce starts to bubble, leave it over the heat for 2 minutes, stirring a little faster to prevent bits from sticking to the bottom. Taste and adjust the seasoning to your liking, then turn off the heat. Your béchamel should be velvety smooth and creamy.

VARIATION
To make a Mornay sauce, as soon as the béchamel is done, stir in 2 large egg yolks and ½ cup (50 g) of grated Gruyère or Comté cheese.

EASY BÉARNAISE

The iconic béarnaise is an essential sauce to add to your cooking repertoire and is typically served with grilled meat and fish. A good béarnaise should have the consistency of mayonnaise. This is a sharp, tarragon-flavored, butter-based sauce combined with a reduction of shallots, wine and vinegar.

Makes ¾ cup (200 ml)

7 oz (200 g) unsalted butter

⅓ cup (80 ml) dry white wine

3 tbsp (45 ml) tarragon vinegar or white wine vinegar

3 tbsp (30 g) diced shallot

2 tbsp (10 g) finely chopped fresh tarragon

1 tsp freshly ground pepper

1 cup (250 ml) water + 1 tsp cold water, divided

3 large egg yolks

Salt, to season

2 tsp (3 g) chopped fresh tarragon, to finish

½ tbsp (3 g) chopped fresh chervil, to finish

MISE EN PLACE

To clarify the butter, melt it in a small saucepan over low heat or use a microwave. Skim off the foam sitting on the surface, then slowly scoop out the clear part of the butter (butterfat) into a bowl and set aside.

To make the reduction, in a small saucepan, combine the wine, vinegar, shallot, tarragon and pepper. Bring it to a boil, then lower the heat slightly and reduce until roughly 1½ teaspoons (8 ml) of liquid remains. Pour the reduction into a large glass bowl sitting over a small saucepan containing 1 cup (250 ml) of the water. (Make sure the bowl doesn't touch the water.) Bring the water to a light simmer over medium-high heat.

Add the egg yolks and the 1 teaspoon of cold water to the reduction and whisk constantly for 5 minutes, or until the mixture doubles in volume and sticks to the whisk when lifted out of the bowl. When done, the mixture should have a thick and creamy consistency.

Transfer the bowl to your countertop to finish the sauce. While the clarified butter is still lukewarm at around 68°F (20°C)—if not, warm it up a little—add a few tablespoons (about 45 ml) at a time, whisking constantly, until fully incorporated before adding more. When done, the sauce should have a thick consistency resembling that of mayonnaise. Now, taste the sauce and season to your liking with the salt. Optionally, stir in an extra ½ teaspoon of vinegar if you prefer a sharper sauce. To finish, stir in the tarragon and the chervil before serving lukewarm.

TIP

If the sauce becomes too thick, whisk in 1 to 2 teaspoons (5 to 10 ml) of warm water to thin out the sauce.

NO-FUSS HOLLANDAISE

This recipe is a simplified version of the classic hollandaise sauce, adjusted to perfectly suit the busy home cook who delights in making things from scratch without spending hours in the kitchen. This modern hollandaise doesn't require a vinegar reduction or clarified butter, and everything is prepared in one bowl. If you've ever wanted to make a hollandaise sauce from scratch for eggs Benedict but felt intimidated by the technical pressure, this is the recipe for you. It's simple, it works, but above all, it tastes great.

Makes ¾ cup (200 ml)

1 cup (250 ml) water
2 large egg yolks
2 tsp (10 ml) white vinegar
5.5 oz (150 g) unsalted butter, at room temperature, cut into medium-sized cubes
2 tbsp (30 ml) fresh lemon juice
Salt and freshly ground pepper, to season
Small pinch of cayenne pepper

MISE EN PLACE
Get your trusted whisk ready because this sauce requires slow, continuous whisking from beginning 'til end.

Fill a small saucepan with the water and bring it to a simmer. Sit a large glass bowl on top of the saucepan, making sure the bowl doesn't touch the water. In the glass bowl, combine the egg yolks and vinegar and whisk together for 30 seconds to start the emulsion. While whisking, drop two or three cubes of butter into the bowl. Continue to whisk until the butter melts before adding another two or three cubes. Repeat until half of the butter is used and the sauce starts to thicken.

Now, you'll need to multitask by gradually whisking in the lemon juice, 1 teaspoon at a time, along with the rest of the butter, two or three cubes at a time. When all the butter and lemon are incorporated, taste the sauce and adjust the seasoning, and whisk in the cayenne. Remove the bowl from the heat and spoon the sauce into a dish, ready to serve.

TIP
The process of making this sauce takes 5 minutes from when you begin whisking. Set a timer to know roughly when the sauce should be ready.

NOTE
Enjoy with poached eggs with smoked salmon or ham (eggs Benedict), poached white fish and salmon or alongside steamed vegetables, such as asparagus or artichokes.

VARIATION
Mousseline sauce is an easy variant of hollandaise sauce. To add it to your sauce-making repertoire, just mix 3 tablespoons (45 ml) of whipped cream into the finished hollandaise.

CHICKEN VELOUTÉ SAUCE

Also known as the *sauce suprême*, this chicken velouté sauce is enriched with cream, mushrooms and a touch of lemon zest for some zing. While it may sound modest on paper, this all-time French classic will take you by surprise for two reasons: it has a taste that punches well above its weight, and it's insanely easy to make. Preparing this sauce is also a great opportunity to road test the White Chicken Stock (page 12) and experience just how much flavor a homemade stock can bring to a sauce.

Makes 1 cup (250 ml)

For the Sautéed Mushrooms
2 tbsp (30 g) unsalted butter
5 button mushrooms, sliced
Salt and freshly ground pepper, to season

For the Velouté
1 oz (30 g) butter
1 oz (30 g) all-purpose flour
2 cups (500 ml) White Chicken Stock (page 12)
1/3 cup (80 ml) heavy cream
1 tsp fresh lemon juice
Pinch of cayenne pepper
Pinch of freshly grated nutmeg
Extra dab of butter, to finish
Pinch of chopped fresh parsley, to finish

MISE EN PLACE

Make the White Chicken Stock in advance according to the recipe on page 12.

In a medium-sized skillet, melt the butter over medium heat and sauté the mushrooms, with a pinch of salt and pepper, until golden. Set aside.

To make the velouté, in a small saucepan, melt the butter over low heat, then stir in the flour and cook for 3 minutes to make what's called a blond roux (mixture of butter and flour). Turn off the heat and allow to cool completely.

In a separate small saucepan, bring the stock to a boil. Turn off the heat, add half of the stock to the roux, whisking gently until you get a thick, lump-free sauce, and then stir in the remaining stock. Bring the velouté to a boil over medium heat, whisking from time to time, until it thickens.

Add the mushrooms and the cream and reduce the sauce for 8 to 10 minutes, stirring occasionally. Add the lemon juice, cayenne and nutmeg and taste. Adjust the seasoning to your liking before switching off the heat. For a final touch, stir in a dab of butter and a pinch of parsley before serving.

NOTE
This sauce pairs beautifully with white meats, such as chicken, turkey, pork or veal.

VARIATION
Create even more flavor by adding either 1 tablespoon (5 g) of finely chopped fresh tarragon or 2 tablespoons (15 g) of capers (in brine) just before serving.

GARDEN-FRESH TOMATO SAUCE

The *nouvelle cuisine* movement during the 1970s introduced the world to a lighter style of French cooking. Since then, the old-style version of tomato sauce gradually fell out of favor as a new generation of French chefs ditched the flour and bacon for fresh tomatoes and herbs. I'm also a convert! This light tomato sauce recipe brings the fresh tomato flavor to the forefront, while the aromatic elements sit fragrantly in the background. It tastes like a summer's garden and can be used in any recipe calling for a tomato sauce or coulis.

Makes 2 cups (500 ml)

2 tbsp (30 g) unsalted butter

1 tbsp (15 ml) olive oil

1 white onion or 2 small shallots, finely diced

1 sprig thyme

1 bay leaf

2 cloves garlic, halved and bruised

2 lb (1 kg) ripe tomatoes, cut in half, seeded and chopped into medium-sized chunks

2 tbsp (30 g) tomato paste

1 tsp (5 g) sugar

¾ cup (200 ml) water

Salt and freshly ground pepper, to season

In a large saucepan over low heat, combine the butter, olive oil, onion, thyme, bay leaf and garlic. Gently mix together with a wooden spoon and cook uncovered for 5 minutes. Add the tomato chunks, tomato paste and sugar and cook for 2 minutes to reduce the acidity of the tomatoes, then add the water, salt and pepper. Give the tomatoes a gentle stir, then simmer, uncovered, for 30 minutes. (Using low heat is key to maintaining the fresh flavor of the tomatoes.)

Pour the tomatoes into a large coarse-mesh sieve or vegetable mill over a bowl or saucepan. Press the tomatoes through, extracting as much juice as possible. Taste and adjust the seasoning to your liking. Use immediately or keep in the fridge for up to 48 hours.

NOTE
This sauce can be served hot or cold as an accompaniment to fish, vegetables or pasta, or used as a saucy base for other recipes.

VARIATION
Add 1 tablespoon (5 g) of chopped fresh herbs at the last minute, for more fragrance.

MOREL MUSHROOM SAUCE
WITH MADEIRA WINE

If, like me, you can't afford truffles, then morels are the next best thing—and much less costly. They're easy to source, and even the dehydrated version tastes exceptional when added to dishes. This recipe is a classic French sauce that, while easy to make, will bring a wow factor to any panfried, roasted or grilled chicken with its intense and lightly sweet flavor.

Makes ¾ cup (200 ml)

For the Morels

2 tbsp (30 g) butter

1 oz (30 g) dried morel mushrooms

1½ tbsp (15 g) finely diced shallot

1 tbsp (3 g) finely chopped fresh parsley

For the Sauce

1¼ cups (300 ml) Homestyle Demi-Glace (page 15)

2 tbsp (30 g) butter

3 tbsp (30 g) finely diced shallot

3 small button mushrooms, finely sliced

½ cup (120 ml) medium-dry Madeira or ruby port wine, plus more to finish

3 tbsp (45 ml) heavy cream

Salt and freshly ground pepper, to season

MISE EN PLACE

Soak the dried morels in 1 cup (250 ml) of boiling water and let them rehydrate for 30 minutes. When rehydrated, drain the morels, wash them thoroughly under cold water and then pat them dry. Slice the larger ones (if any) and leave the small ones whole.

Make the Homestyle Demi-Glace in advance according to the recipe on page 15.

In a small skillet, melt the butter over medium heat and panfry the morels and shallot for 3 minutes. Sprinkle with the parsley, mixing well, and set aside.

To make the sauce, in a medium-sized saucepan, melt the butter over medium heat. When the butter foams, add the shallot and the mushrooms and cook, stirring regularly, for 3 minutes, or until the mushrooms are lightly colored. Pour in the Madeira wine and reduce until 3 to 4 tablespoons (45 to 60 ml) of liquid are left in the pan. Follow by adding the demi-glace and reduce at a light boil for 10 minutes.

When ready, stir in the morel mixture and the cream, then lower the heat to medium and cook until the sauce is thick enough to coat the back of a spoon (about 5 minutes). To finish, taste and adjust the seasoning, then to boost the flavor, add a dash of Madeira wine. *Et voilà*, your sauce is ready.

BURGUNDY-STYLE RED WINE SAUCE

This versatile red wine sauce is derived from an old-fashioned branch of French cuisine called *la cuisine de ménage*, which we know today as home cooking. In the early 20th century, this was the go-to sauce for busy French women juggling the demands of running a household and wanting to impress with their cooking. It's rich and flavorful, and oozes depth with the addition of a full-bodied red wine. Although it goes well with almost every type of meat, I also recommend it poured over poached eggs to re-create Burgundy's famous *œufs en meurette*.

Makes 1 cup (250 ml)

For the Sauce

¾ cup (200 ml) Homestyle Demi-Glace (page 15)

2 tbsp (30 g) unsalted butter

1 onion, finely diced

1 medium-sized carrot, finely diced

4 button mushrooms, finely chopped

3.5 oz (100 g) smoked bacon, sliced into medium-sized strips (lardons)

1½ cups (350 ml) good-quality, full-bodied red wine

1 clove garlic, bruised

1 sprig thyme

1 small bay leaf

½ tsp whole peppercorns

For the Garnish

2 tbsp (30 g) butter, divided

2 oz (60 g) smoked bacon, sliced into medium-sized strips (lardons)

3 button mushrooms, quartered

Salt and pepper, to season

1 tbsp (3 g) chopped fresh parsley

A dash of cognac (optional)

MISE EN PLACE
Make the Homestyle Demi-Glace in advance according to the recipe on page 15.

To make the sauce, in a medium-sized saucepan, melt the butter over low heat and stir in the onion, carrot, mushrooms and bacon and cook gently for 8 to 10 minutes, stirring occasionally. Pour in the wine and add the garlic, thyme, bay leaf and peppercorns. Bring to a boil and let the wine reduce for 12 minutes, or until reduced by roughly two-thirds.

Add the demi-glace, and then return to a light boil before reducing the sauce for 10 to 15 minutes, depending on how rich you want the sauce to be. When it's ready, the sauce should have a burgundy tinge with an intense red wine flavor. Strain the sauce through a fine-mesh sieve into a separate saucepan and set it aside while you prepare the garnish.

To make the garnish, in a medium-sized skillet, heat 1 tablespoon (15 g) of the butter and panfry the bacon and mushrooms until golden, then scrape the mixture into the sauce. Just before serving, bring the sauce to a simmer then remove from the heat. To finish, stir in the remaining butter, season to taste with the salt and pepper and sprinkle in the parsley. For a touch of class and to take the edge off the acidity of the wine, add a dash of cognac, if you wish. Serve immediately.

MASCARPONE WHIPPED CREAM

Aside from being rich and luxurious, the great thing about mascarpone whipped cream
is that it keeps well at room temperature for a long time. This feature makes it the perfect
candidate for decorating and filling cakes or choux puffs, and as a topping on fruits or ice cream.
Of course, you can use the same measurements in this recipe to make a classic
whipped cream without the mascarpone.

Makes 1 cup (250 g)

¾ cup (200 ml) heavy cream

1 oz (30 g) powdered sugar

1 rounded tbsp (20 g)
mascarpone cheese

1 tsp vanilla extract (optional)

MISE EN PLACE

The cream and mascarpone
must be cold, ideally having
spent the night in the fridge.
Chill the bowl for whipping
the cream in the freezer for at
least 15 minutes before you
start. Get your stand or hand
mixer ready. If you don't mind
using some elbow grease, you
can whip the cream by hand
with a large balloon whisk.

Combine the cream, sugar and mascarpone cheese in a bowl and
whip on low speed for 2 minutes to allow the sugar to dissolve
and the mascarpone to blend with the cream. After 2 minutes,
increase the speed to medium, taking care not to go too fast to avoid
overwhipping the cream. Keep an eye on the consistency, and stop
whisking when you see prominent swirls as you whisk and the
cream starts to stiffen. If using vanilla extract, gently fold it in with a
spatula. From here, spoon the cream into a piping bag and decorate
away or use a spoon to dollop onto cakes and desserts.

TIP

For an even stiffer cream, increase the amount of mascarpone to
2 tablespoons (30 g). However, this is best reserved for cakes and
desserts displayed at room temperature for long periods of time.

TRADITIONAL FRENCH MERINGUE

With its sweet, crumbly texture and gooey interior, I confess that I have a small meringue addiction. I'll make a batch whenever I have some extra egg whites, just for nibbling on throughout the day like a mouse. There are three techniques to make meringue: the Italian, the Swiss and the French, and I'm pleased to reveal that the French method is the quickest and easiest for a variety of uses in home baking.

Makes 20 small or 10 medium-sized meringues

4.4 oz (125 g) powdered sugar

5.3 oz (150 g) granulated sugar, divided

5.3 oz (150 g) egg whites from 5 eggs

¼ tsp lemon juice

MISE EN PLACE

You'll need a stand or hand mixer and a piping bag fitted with a tip of your choice.

In a bowl, mix the powdered sugar with 4.5 oz (125 g) of the granulated sugar, and set the rest of the granulated sugar aside. Preheat the oven to 195°F (90°C). Line a baking sheet with parchment paper.

Combine the egg whites with the lemon juice in the mixing bowl and whisk on medium speed for 3 minutes, or until the egg whites double in volume. Without stopping the mixer, add the reserved granulated sugar and whisk for 2 minutes. Now start to slowly pour in the powdered and granulated sugar mixture, whisking for 2 minutes, or until the meringue becomes stiff and glossy.

Meringue needs to be cooked as soon as it's prepared, so immediately fill the piping bag with the meringue and pipe your desired shapes onto the baking sheet, leaving 1 inch (2.5 cm) between each meringue. Bake for 2 hours (or up to 3 hours for large meringue), then remove from the oven and allow to rest for at least 30 minutes before detaching them. Eat right away or use to decorate your desserts.

TIPS

Make sure the egg whites are free of even a speck of yolk. This is important to ensure the meringue rises properly.

You can add all sorts of extra ingredients to the meringue, but never anything more than 3 tablespoons (25 g). Dried or candied fruit, toasted almonds and pink praline all work well.

CRÊPES

Ask a French person whether they prefer caviar or crêpes, and they'll likely answer "crêpes" without hesitation. These thin pancakes are enjoyed by everybody in France, not just the kids. Every time I reach for my crêpe pan, I'm flooded with childhood memories of watching, with anticipation, the crêpe stack growing taller while counting the various ways I would eat each one: the first with sugar, the second with jam and cream, the third with a chocolate spread and so on. I have experimented with many recipes over the years to land on this one for the perfect crêpes.

Makes 15 crêpes, using a 10" (25-cm) crêpe pan

8.8 oz (250 g) all-purpose flour
Pinch of salt
2 tsp (10 g) sugar
3 large eggs
2½ cups (600 ml) whole milk, divided
1.8 oz (50 g) unsalted butter
1 tbsp (15 ml) liquor, dark rum or Grand Marnier® (optional)
3 tbsp (45 ml) cooking oil

MISE EN PLACE
You will need a crêpe pan or nonstick skillet.

In a large bowl, whisk together the flour, salt and sugar, and then make a well in the middle. Break the eggs and pour them into the well. To prevent clumps in the batter, first add 1 cup (250 ml) of the milk to the well and whisk until the batter is lump-free and smooth. Then, pour in a second cup (250 ml) and whisk until the batter is smooth again.

Cover the bowl with a clean tea towel, and let the batter rest at room temperature for at least 1 hour. (If you're patient, 2 hours is best.) Stir in the remaining milk, then pass the batter through a sieve into a bowl to ensure the batter is completely lump-free.

Melt the butter in a small saucepan, or briefly in a microwave, and whisk it into the batter along with the liquor (if using), and voilà, you're ready to cook some crêpes.

The key to cooking the perfect crêpe is to use just enough batter to cover the bottom of the pan and no more (roughly 3 tablespoons [45 ml] per crepe). First, grease and heat the pan over medium-high heat, then drop a scoop of batter in and swirl the pan to spread the batter evenly. Cook the first side for up to a minute until golden, flip, and repeat for the second side. Slide the crêpe onto a plate and repeat, oiling the pan between adding batter, until all the batter is gone. Enjoy with your favorite toppings.

ALL-PURPOSE SHORT CRUST

If you want to make a short crust without breaking a sweat, then give this recipe a try. Contrary to what people think, making short crust pastry by hand is straightforward and fast. This recipe is a classic from culinary schools and yields a perfect result every time. The dough is easy to roll out, which is great for building confidence in working with pastry. Even better, this dough can be made with or without sugar, making it suitable for both sweet and savory delights, such as quiches, fruit tarts and custard flan.

Makes 1 lb (500 g) (enough to fit a 10" [25-cm]-diameter tart pan)

8.8 oz (250 g) all-purpose flour, sifted, plus more to dust the work surface

4.4 oz (125 g) unsalted butter, fridge cold and cut into small cubes

0.7 oz (20 g) egg yolk from 1 medium-sized egg

3 tbsp + 1 tsp (50 ml) cold water

1 tsp salt

MISE EN PLACE

Measure the ingredients precisely, especially the egg yolk, which must be exactly 0.7 ounce (20 grams).

Place the flour in a large glass bowl, then disperse the cubed butter over it. Now, get ready for a bit of a workout. Firmly grab and squeeze handfuls of flour and butter to start mixing them together, and then follow by rubbing the flour and butter between your fingertips. Work fast to avoid warming the mixture and you should end up with a coarse and sandy mixture with minimal lumps.

In a small bowl, combine the egg yolk, water and salt, and stir gently with a fork until the salt has completely dissolved. Pour the egg yolk mixture evenly over the flour mixture and use a fork to stir together. Stop as soon as you have a cohesive dough that comes together when pressed in your palm. Gather the dough to make a rough ball shape.

Dust your countertop with a pinch or two of flour, then plonk the dough on the bench and use your hands to gather and roll it into a smooth ball. Knead the dough by spreading it flat with the palm of your hand, using a firm downward motion in different directions until the dough is flat. To finish, gather the dough back into a ball again and flatten it into a thick disk. Wrap it in plastic wrap and let it rest in the fridge for at least 2 hours.

Remove the short crust dough from the fridge at least 30 minutes before you use it for a recipe. This prevents cracks from forming in the dough and makes it more malleable and easier to roll.

NOTE

To save time, you can use a food processor to process the flour and butter cubes for up to 1 minute, or until you have a sandy mixture. Use again to process the sandy mixture with the liquid ingredients for roughly 1 minute, or until a ball of dough forms.

VARIATION

To make a sweet short crust, add 1 tablespoon (13 g) of granulated sugar when you combine the egg yolk, water and salt. This sweet version is suitable for blind baking and great for fruit tarts.

PASTRY CREAM

When it comes to French desserts, I don't think there is anything tastier or more versatile than a pastry cream. Although this thick custard is used to fill pastries like choux puffs, éclairs and to spread between layers of sponge cake, I know people who eat it straight out of the bowl (no judgment here). This recipe oozes natural vanilla flavor and takes 30 minutes to prepare.

Makes 1 lb (500 g)

2 cups (500 ml) whole milk

1 vanilla bean, split in half lengthwise with the seeds scraped

3.5 oz (100 g) egg yolks (from 5 large eggs)

4.2 oz (120 g) sugar

1 oz (30 g) cornstarch

1 oz (30 g) all-purpose flour

1 tbsp (15 g) unsalted butter, cut into small cubes

In a small saucepan, combine the milk and the vanilla bean with the seeds. Bring to a simmer over medium heat, stirring from time to time. Meanwhile, in a large glass bowl, vigorously whisk together the egg yolks and sugar for 1 minute, or until the sugar is dissolved. Sift in the cornstarch and flour and whisk again, this time gently, until you get a thick paste.

By now, the milk should be warm enough, so let's make the custard. First, pour one-quarter of the milk (½ cup [120 ml]) through a sieve into the egg mixture and whisk gently until the mixture is lump-free. Then, stir in the rest of the milk and remove the vanilla pod. Strain the custard through a sieve into the same saucepan used to warm the milk. Place it over medium heat, stirring constantly with a whisk so that the custard gradually thickens into a pastry cream. As soon as it starts to thicken, whisk faster to prevent heavy lumps from forming.

When the pastry cream starts to boil, turn the heat to low and cook for 2 minutes, whisking vigorously so that nothing sticks to the bottom of the pan. Turn off the heat and let it cool for a few minutes before mixing in the butter until it's fully incorporated. Transfer the pastry cream to a baking pan, flattening and smoothing the top with a spatula. Cover with plastic wrap in direct contact with the pastry cream to prevent a crust from forming on the top, then chill for at least 2 hours in the refrigerator to allow the flavor to fully develop.

NOTE
Pastry cream is best used the day it is made, as it tends to lose its flavor after 24 hours.

VARIATIONS
When using the pastry cream for a dessert, spoon it into a large bowl with 1 tablespoon (15 ml) of white rum or Grand Marnier and whisk vigorously to bring the creamy consistency back.

For a more indulgent filling for choux puffs and éclairs, fold in ¼ cup (60 ml) of whipped cream just after adding the liquor.

CHOUX PASTRY

Be it baking or cooking, choux pastry is a staple in French cuisine, appearing in dozens of sweet and savory recipes. While the thought of making choux pastry from scratch triggers feelings of apprehension in many, using precise measurements and the right technique will reveal there's no reason to fear choux.

Makes 25 choux puffs

For the Choux Pastry
4.2 fl oz (125 ml) water
4.2 fl oz (125 ml) whole milk
3.5 oz (100 g) unsalted butter, cut into small cubes
½ tsp salt
2½ tsp (12.5 g) sugar
5.3 oz (150 g) all-purpose flour
8.5 oz (240 g) beaten egg (from 5 large eggs), at room temperature
3 tbsp (25 g) powdered sugar, to sprinkle over the choux

MISE EN PLACE
You will need a piping bag fitted with a straight tip to pipe the choux. You can use a stand mixer fitted with a paddle attachment to mix the dough or mix by hand using a bowl and a wooden spoon. Preheat the oven (conventional oven or with fan turned off) to 430°F (220°C). Line a baking sheet with parchment paper.

In a medium-sized saucepan, combine the water, milk, butter, salt and sugar and bring to a boil, stirring constantly to help the butter melt into the liquid. As soon as the liquid starts to boil, turn off the heat and add the flour all at once. Stir with a wooden spoon to form a ball of dough and mix constantly until it becomes smooth.

Place the pan back over medium heat and stir constantly for 1 minute, or until the dough becomes smooth and shiny and a film forms at the bottom of the pan. Transfer the dough to the stand mixer bowl and stir the dough for 1 minute on medium speed. (This is necessary to release excess heat in the dough.)

Add one-third of the beaten eggs at a time to the dough (still on medium speed) waiting until each portion of egg is fully incorporated before adding the next. When done, the batter should be smooth and glossy.

To lay the choux, spoon the dough into the piping bag and hold it firmly in a vertical position to pipe walnut-sized mounds onto the baking sheet, leaving a 1½-inch (4-cm) space between the mounds. For éclairs, pipe the mixture into 5-inch (13-cm)-long lines. Use a fork dipped in water to flatten the pointy top of each choux, and then sprinkle with the powdered sugar.

Lower the oven temperature to 375°F (190°C) and immediately slide the pan of choux into the oven. Bake for 30 minutes, or until golden brown. (No matter what happens, never open the oven door while the choux are cooking!) When cooked, leave the choux to rest on a cooling rack before serving.

VARIATION
For the savory version used to make Gougères (page 55), follow the same process but with the following ingredients:

8.4 fl oz (250 ml) water
3.5 oz (100 g) unsalted butter
½ tsp salt
5.3 oz (150 g) all-purpose flour
8.5 oz (240 g) beaten egg (from 5 large eggs), at room temperature

Part 2: To Start

SMALL BITES FOR ALL OCCASIONS

In France, much is contemplated over an afternoon aperitif with friends. Whiling away the twilight hours with a tasty snack and a predinner drink is all part of our *joie de vivre*. There is something in the French DNA that makes this ritual look effortless. I like to call it the hosting gene. Whether prearranged or unexpected, a visit is always met with an offer of *pastis* (an anise-flavored liqueur) or a glass of wine, accompanied by delicious snacks. The trick is to serve something not too small, but not too substantial either . . . just enough to whet the appetite for a heavier meal ahead. The small bites here are a combination of make-ahead and entertaining tidbits to cater for both the planned drop-in and the unannounced guest. From a simple Tapenade (page 47) that can be tucked away in the fridge days ahead, to a Tomato and Mustard Feuilleté (page 56) ready in under 45 minutes, these simple recipes will help remove any anxiety attached to impromptu entertaining and work just as well for brunch as for cocktail parties.

TAPENADE

As soon as summer hits, tapenade pops up everywhere in market stalls across Provence. We affectionately refer to this black olive spread as "the poor man's caviar," but there is nothing poor about the experience of biting into toasted baguette topped with a layer of fresh black olive goodness in between sips of a Côtes de Provence rosé. This dip is simple to make and has so many uses: served on toasted bread during aperitif drinks, as a filling for a crudité sandwich or as a dip with raw vegetables. Olives are the star of the show in this recipe, so it pays to use the best-quality olives you can find.

Serves 4–6

1¹/₃ cups (250 g) unflavored black olives

2 oz (60 g) anchovy filets in oil, drained and patted dry

3 tbsp (25 g) drained and patted dry capers in brine

½ clove garlic, crushed in a garlic press

2 tbsp (30 ml) olive oil, plus extra for topping

2 generous pinches of freshly ground pepper

MISE EN PLACE

You can use pitted olives, but olives with stones bring a richer flavor. If using unpitted olives, use a pitter to remove the pits. If using pitted olives in brine, drain and pat the olives dry. Set up your food processor with a standard knife blade.

In the food processor, combine the olives, anchovies, capers and garlic. Add the oil and pepper and process for 3 minutes, or until the mixture becomes a spreadable paste. Spoon the tapenade into a glass jar and top with a thin layer of olive oil, then store in the fridge. If you want to serve it now, let the tapenade rest in a serving dish for at least 30 minutes to allow the flavors to develop.

TIP
Keep in the fridge for several days, ready for immediate consumption whenever the occasion calls for it.

EGGS MIMOSA

This classic hors d'oeuvre is the spice-free French version of deviled eggs, where a hard-boiled egg is cut in half, the yolk is mashed and mixed with mayonnaise and then spooned back into the egg. The term "mimosa" refers to the decorative element on top that imitates the look of a mimosa flower, the first sign of spring in France. This is created by pressing the cooked egg yolk through a sieve and sprinkling it, petal-like, over the stuffed eggs.

Makes 8 eggs mimosa

¼ cup (60 ml) Homemade Mayonnaise (page 22)

5 large eggs

1 tbsp (5 g) finely chopped fresh chives

Salt and freshly ground pepper to garnish (optional)

MISE EN PLACE

Make the Homemade Mayonnaise according to the recipe on page 22.

Cook the eggs in boiling water for 9 minutes, then let them sit in cold water for 10 minutes before peeling them. Use a sharp knife to cut the eggs in half and delicately remove the yolks. Place 7 of the yolk halves in a bowl and set the other 3 aside for the decorative element.

To make the filling, use a fork to press the yolks in the bowl and slowly incorporate the mayonnaise until you get a smooth mixture.

To make the decorative element, press the remaining 3 yolk halves through a sieve into a small bowl. Spoon the egg filling into the white egg halves and garnish with a smattering of the pressed yolks and a sprinkle of chives and salt and pepper, if using. Arrange the eggs mimosa on a dish and serve.

VARIATION

If you can't resist, tap a few drops of Tabasco into the egg and mayonnaise mixture to add heat to your mimosas.

BAKED EGGS WITH TOMATO, CAPERS AND CROUTONS

During my teenage years, I lived for a short while in a small town on the French Riviera just fifteen minutes from the Italian border. This is where I discovered a local specialty called *œufs pizzaiolo*, a Franco-Italian starter baked in wood-fired ovens in pizzerias across the Riviera. I've always loved this recipe for its simplicity and clever use of ingredients. The formula is simple: baked eggs on a bed of herb-infused passata, with a sprinkle of capers for zing and a drizzle of olive oil. The dish was always served piping hot, topped with croutons for a light crunch. It's proof that the French and Italians can make beautiful things together.

Serves 2

2 tbsp (30 g) unsalted butter

2 slices baguette-style bread, cut into small cubes

2 tbsp (30 ml) olive oil, plus more to drizzle

Salt and pepper, to season

½ cup (120 ml) freshly made (page 29) or top-quality tomato sauce with herbs, divided

4 large eggs

2 tbsp (20 g) capers in brine

MISE EN PLACE

Preheat the oven to 425°F (220°C) in preparation to cook the eggs quickly.

To make the croutons, melt the butter over medium heat and panfry the bread cubes until golden brown. Set aside.

Coat the bottom of two small, shallow ovenproof dishes with the olive oil, followed by a pinch of salt and pepper and 2 tablespoons (30 g) of tomato sauce.

Break the eggs directly into the dishes (2 eggs per dish), then sprinkle the capers evenly over the egg whites, avoiding the yolk. Finish by spooning the rest of the tomato sauce on top along with a drizzle of olive oil. Again, avoid touching the yolks.

Bake the eggs on the middle rack of the oven for 5 to 10 minutes, or until the whites are just set and the yolks are still runny (or to your taste). When cooked, top with a handful of croutons and serve immediately.

GREEK-STYLE MUSHROOMS

This dish was king of salad bars in the 1980s and was so ubiquitous across France that I remember it featured regularly on my school's dining menu. Over the years, it has unfortunately faded into obscurity, but for no good reason. Served lukewarm or cold, the pickled mushrooms flavored with tomato, wine, onion, spices and a touch of lemon juice deliver a punchy tang that takes you by surprise. Let's bring this retro dish back to life!

Serves 4

For the Bouquet Garni
1 clove garlic
1 sprig thyme
½ bay leaf
10 coriander seeds
10 peppercorns

For the Mushrooms
2 tbsp (30 ml) olive oil, plus more for serving
½ onion, finely chopped
10.5 oz (300 g) button mushrooms, stalks removed and caps quartered
Juice of 1 lemon, plus more for serving
3 tbsp (45 ml) white wine
½ tsp salt, plus more to season
1 tbsp (15 ml) tomato paste
2 tbsp (20 g) canned diced tomatoes
1 tsp sugar
Freshly ground pepper

MISE EN PLACE
To make the bouquet garni, lay the ingredients on a small square of cheesecloth and tie the top with kitchen twine. This allows the aromatics to slowly infuse when cooking the mushrooms, and then it's easily discarded after cooking.

In a medium-sized saucepan, heat the oil and sauté the onion over medium heat for 3 minutes, stirring regularly to ensure the onion stays translucent. Add the mushrooms, mixing them gently with the onion, then add the lemon juice and wine, and mix again. Sprinkle with the salt and simmer for 5 minutes to release the moisture from the mushrooms.

Stir in the tomato paste, diced tomatoes and sugar, and bury the bouquet garni under the mushrooms. Simmer, partially covered, for 15 minutes, or until the cooking juices have reduced and become almost syrupy. To finish, remove the bouquet garni and adjust the seasoning with salt and pepper. Transfer to a dish and let it cool at room temperature for 30 minutes before serving with a splash of olive oil and lemon juice. Best enjoyed heaped onto a slice of toasted baguette.

GOUGÈRES

Gougères, originally a Burgundian specialty, have become a timeless predinner nibble enjoyed across France. These fluffy nuggets of goodness are made of a simple choux pastry filled with cheese and baked to be devoured with your favorite people. Now, don't be put off by the mention of choux pastry. This recipe is easy to make and a fun opportunity to perfect your choux-making skills.

Makes 15 gougères

1 batch savory Choux Pastry dough (see variation on page 43)

Pinch of freshly ground pepper

Pinch of freshly grated nutmeg

5.5 oz (150 g) Gruyère or Comté cheese

Egg wash

MISE EN PLACE

You will need a piping bag fitted with a large straight tip to pipe the gougères. Make the savory Choux Pastry dough according to the recipe variation on page 43. Grate half of the cheese and cut the other half into small cubes. Mix 1 egg yolk with 1 tsp water to make the egg wash. Preheat the oven (conventional oven or with fan turned off) to 425°F (220°C). Line a baking sheet with parchment paper.

Once you have prepared the choux pastry dough, add the pepper and nutmeg, followed by both the grated and cubed cheese to the dough. (Reserve a small amount of grated cheese for garnish.) Give the dough a vigorous stir to ensure the ingredients are distributed evenly throughout.

Load the dough into the piping bag and hold it firmly in a vertical position to pipe walnut-sized mounds onto the baking sheet, leaving 1½ inches (4 cm) of space between the mounds. To finish, brush the tops with egg wash and garnish with a pinch of grated cheese.

Lower the oven temperature to 350°F (180°C).

Immediately slide the baking sheet into the oven. Bake for 30 to 40 minutes, or until well puffed and golden brown. (Don't open the door while the gougères are baking, to avoid the disappointment of deflation.)

Gougères are made to be shared, so serve on a tray, in a small basket or on a cake stand, for a fancier look. They really shine when nibbled between sips of a white Burgundy-style wine.

VARIATION

Add all sorts of ingredients to the dough to change it up. Experiment with different types of cheese or try adding bacon, ham or herbs.

TOMATO AND MUSTARD FEUILLETÉ

Meet your new all-purpose dish for summer entertaining. When friends are coming over for a spontaneous aperitif, this puff pastry tart is my go-to recipe. It's quick and easy and will be devoured by guests at any type of gathering, from garden party to family lunch on a sunny terrace. What I love most about this recipe is that no tart or pie dish is required. Just roll out the premade puff pastry and top with the condiments, herbs and juicy ripe tomatoes.
It's like a slice of Provence on your plate.

Serves 4–6

1 roll or sheet premade puff pastry

2 tbsp (30 ml) Dijon mustard

4 tbsp (60 ml) plain tomato sauce (page 29) or Italian passata

5 tbsp (40 g) breadcrumbs

5 to 6 large tomatoes, sliced finely

Few pinches of salt

1 tsp freshly ground black pepper

1 tbsp dried herbes de Provence or Italian seasoning

Basil leaves, for garnish

3 tbsp (45 ml) olive oil

MISE EN PLACE

Puff pastry is much easier to work with cold, so remove the pastry sheet from the freezer ahead of time and keep chilled in the fridge at the ready. I use a large pastry sheet, but you can use any size you like. Preheat the oven to 400°F (200°C). Line a baking sheet with parchment paper.

Place the puff pastry on the baking sheet. Fold the edges of the pastry sheet 2 inches (5 cm) inward to mimic the rim of a tart dish. Use a pastry brush to coat the base of the pastry with the mustard, followed by a layer of tomato sauce and a smattering of breadcrumbs, avoiding the folded edges. Arrange the tomato slices in tidy overlapping rows, taking care that none are resting along the edges of the tart. Feel free to cram in as many tomatoes as you can. Sprinkle with salt, pepper, herbes de Provence and basil leaves, plus a generous glug of olive oil.

Bake for 25 to 30 minutes (depending on size), or until the pastry is puffy and golden and the tomatoes are slightly shriveled. Serve cut into slices.

CARAMELIZED ONION AND BACON QUICHE

Would a French cookbook be truly authentic without at least one quiche recipe? Making your first quiche is like a culinary rite of passage in France. I remember standing on a chair to reach the kitchen table, awkwardly rolling out homemade short crust pastry and whisking savory custard with my grandma patiently coaching me on the side. The moment I breathed in the buttery aroma of my quiche cooking in the oven, I was hooked! This recipe is a version of the classic quiche Lorraine, the mother of all quiches, made with bacon, eggs and cream. My personal touch is to use caramelized onions, which add a lovely, soft sweetness.

Serves 4 to 6 (enough for 10¼-inch [26-cm] tart pan)

For the Crust
1 batch of All-Purpose Short Crust (page 39) or a roll of premade short crust

For the Garnish
2 tbsp (30 g) unsalted butter

2 medium onions, sliced finely

2 tsp (10 g) sugar

9 oz (250 g) smoked bacon (whole piece), cut into medium-sized strips (lardons)

For the Savory Custard
4 large eggs

1 cup (250 ml) whole milk

1 cup (250 ml) heavy cream

Salt and pepper, to season

Pinch of freshly ground nutmeg

TIP
Never attempt to slice or unmold a quiche straight out of the oven unless you want to risk the disappointment of it breaking apart. To ensure the filling holds firm, let it cool at room temperature for 2 hours before slicing and serving.

MISE EN PLACE
Make the short crust according to the recipe on page 39, or have a roll of premade short crust at the ready. Line the quiche pan with the rolled-out short crust, and then chill in the fridge for at least 15 minutes to allow the dough to firm. (This prevents the dough from shrinking when baking in the oven.) Preheat the oven to 400°F (200°C).

To prepare the garnish, in a skillet, melt the butter over medium-high heat, and then add the onions and sugar. Cook for 15 minutes, stirring often, until the onions become golden. Transfer the onions to a bowl and set aside. Using the same pan and without adding any extra fat, panfry the bacon lardons over medium heat until crisp and lightly browned. Transfer the bacon to a paper towel–lined plate to drain.

To make the savory custard, in a large bowl, beat the eggs, then pour in the milk and cream, whisking gently to combine the ingredients. Season with a little salt (not too much, the bacon is already salty), pepper and nutmeg. Remove the quiche pan from the fridge and sprinkle the bacon and caramelized onions evenly all over the bottom. Gently pour in the custard until the pan is almost full, leaving a small space at the top so that it doesn't overflow when cooking.

Bake the quiche for 30 minutes on the lower oven rack to ensure the bottom of the quiche cooks properly. The cooking time may vary depending on how the oven performs. Set a timer and check the quiche after at least 20 minutes in the oven. When ready, the crust should be fully cooked through and the top lightly browned.

GRAND AIOLI PLATTER

In the south of France, the grand aioli is all about sharing simple food with friends on a sunny day, with a glass of rosé wine in one hand and the other hand free to dip varied morsels in the aioli. This is a flexible affair, as any combination of vegetables and seafood will do, the only rule being that it must be served with a homemade aioli dipping sauce, an olive oil and garlic–based mayonnaise. This recipe includes my easy and foolproof aioli, which also contains a dash of mustard. Serve with a Côtes de Provence rosé or dry white wine.

Serves 4–6

For the Platter

1 lb (500 g) cooked shrimp (optional)

1 small bunch radishes, halved

1 Lebanese cucumber, quartered

Handful of mixed lettuce leaves

10 baby potatoes

1 tbsp (15 g) coarse salt

4 large eggs

1 small cauliflower

1 lb (500 g) broccolini or asparagus

1 bunch spring carrots

For the Aioli

1–2 cloves garlic (depending on how strong you like your aioli to be)

1 tsp Dijon mustard

1 large egg yolk

Salt and pepper, to season

¾ cup (200 ml) olive oil

1 tsp fresh lemon juice

MISE EN PLACE

Shell the shrimp, if needed, and keep in the fridge until ready to serve. Cut and plate the radishes and cucumber, and place the mixed lettuce in a serving bowl. Wash and scrub the mussels to remove any grit stuck to the shells and cut the hairlike seaweed protruding from the clasp of each mussel.

To prepare the platter, place the potatoes in a saucepan filled with cold water and bring to a boil. Add the salt and cook for 20 minutes, or until the flesh of the potatoes is easily pierced with a pointy knife. Drain them and set aside.

While the potatoes are cooking, hard-boil the eggs in boiling water for 10 minutes, then sit them in cold water for 10 minutes before shelling them. Parcook the cauliflower, broccolini and carrots in boiling water for 5 minutes, then rinse under cold water and pat dry.

To make the aioli, use a garlic press to puree the garlic into a large bowl, then add the mustard, egg yolk and a pinch of salt and pepper. Whisk vigorously for 1 minute to start the emulsion. Add the olive oil a little at a time while whisking constantly, until the sauce starts to thicken, then keep on adding a few tablespoons (about 45 ml) of the oil at a time until all of it has been added. By the end, you should have a thick-looking mayonnaise. To finish, stir in the lemon juice and adjust the seasoning, if needed.

For the Mussels

2 lb (1 kg) mussels

2 tbsp (30 g) unsalted butter

3 tbsp (30 g) finely diced shallot

2 tbsp (6 g) chopped fresh parsley

3 tbsp (45 ml) dry white wine

Pinch of freshly ground pepper

To cook the mussels, in a large pot, combine the butter, shallot, parsley, wine and pepper. Bring to a boil, then add the mussels, cover and cook, shaking the pot every few moments. Cook for 4 to 5 minutes, or until most of the mussels have opened.

Assemble the ingredients attractively on a platter or large chopping board and serve with the aioli on the side for easy dipping.

TIMELESS SALADS, SOUPS AND APPETIZERS

Whether it's a salad, soup or appetizer, an *entrée* should never be treated as a filler to pad out a meal; it has the important role of whetting the appetite for what's to come.

Starting with salad, in France, they range from a simple green lettuce mixed with dressing (*salade verte*) all the way to a colorful medley of ingredients (vegetables, meat, fish, cheese or croutons) that almost make for a meal themselves (*salade composée*). From an almost endless list of classic French salads, I've selected some of my personal favorites. They're all easy to make, with each offering a distinctive regional style and taste.

When it comes to soups in French cooking, though they can be served as an entrée, they can be also enjoyed as a comfort dish at any time of day. Like salads, the list of soups you can make is immense. This chapter offers a small selection of soups using different methods to bring interesting textures and tastes to the table.

Whether you're planning a dinner party or looking for a small but exciting meal, the small selection of assorted appetizers here will have you covered. They range from a humble melding of simple ingredients to a classy creation that threatens to steal the show. (We're looking at you, Twice-Baked Cheese and Ham Soufflé with Gourmet Mushrooms [page 100].)

Along the paved roads of the old city of Lyon, you'll find this hearty salad on the menu in the many local eateries known as *bouchons*. Usually served as a side dish to complement the many Lyonnaise specialties, this recipe uses curly endive lettuce leaves, lardons, garlic-panfried croutons, soft-boiled eggs and a drizzle of walnut oil vinaigrette. It can also work as a small meal or as a generous starter for the very hungry. A walnut oil vinaigrette brings the rich nuttiness that this salad is known for, but the Creamy Garlic Vinaigrette (page 18) works well, too.

Serves 4 as a starter or side

2 batches Burgundy-Style Vinaigrette (page 17)

2 large eggs

1 bunch endive lettuce

3.5 oz (100 g) smoked pork belly, rind removed, cut into small strips (lardons)

2 tbsp (30 g) unsalted butter

4 thin slices baguette-style bread

1 clove garlic, halved

MISE EN PLACE

Make the Burgundy-Style Vinaigrette according to recipe on page 17 (double the ingredients to make two batches). This salad can be made with either poached or medium-boiled eggs. I like to use the latter for simplicity and to save time. Cook the eggs in boiling water for 6 minutes, then transfer them to a bowl of cold water to cool for 10 minutes before shelling them. Cut each egg in half. Cut the base off the lettuce and wash and dry the leaves. Trim or discard any damaged salad leaves.

In a dry nonstick pan over medium heat, panfry the pork belly until golden brown, then remove and drain on a paper towel.

To prepare the croutons, melt the butter and panfry the baguette slices in a skillet over medium heat, turning the slices over so that each side is lightly browned. When cooked, use a paper towel to pat dry, and then rub both sides of the slices with the garlic clove.

Place the lettuce in a large bowl, pour half the dressing on top and toss until the leaves shine with the vinaigrette. Divide among serving bowls, scatter with the lardons and croutons, and then arrange the egg halves neatly on top. Finish with a drizzle of the remaining vinaigrette and serve.

FARMHOUSE LENTIL SALAD

Green (du Puy) lentils are protected by a label of guaranteed origin in France. They are grown in a specific region benefiting from a microclimate that gives them their unique taste and texture. The good news is that these iconic pulses can be bought in most countries, and this comfort salad is a hearty way to enjoy them. Cooked until just tender, the lentils are tossed with a Burgundy-style vinaigrette with chives, shallots and a generous sprinkle of lardons.

Serves 4 as a starter

1 batch Burgundy-Style Vinaigrette (page 17)

7 oz (200 g) du Puy lentils (or another variety that will hold firm), rinsed under cold water

2 whole cloves

½ onion

1 qt (1 L) water

½ carrot, sliced

1 bay leaf

1 sprig thyme

5.5 oz (150 g) smoked bacon (whole piece), cut into thick strips (lardons)

2 pinches of salt

1 tbsp (5 g) chopped fresh chives

1 shallot, finely diced

MISE EN PLACE

Make the Burgundy-Style Vinaigrette according to the recipe on page 17. Rinse the lentils in a sieve under running water. Stick the cloves into the onion half.

In a medium-sized saucepan, add the lentils, water, clove-studded onion, carrot, bay leaf and thyme and bring to a boil. Lower the heat and simmer, uncovered, for 25 to 30 minutes, or until the lentils are tender but not mushy.

Meanwhile, in a dry skillet, panfry the lardons until golden brown, then remove and drain on a paper towel.

When the lentils are cooked, scoop out the bay leaf, thyme, carrot and onion and leave the lentils to drain through a sieve for a few minutes. Transfer the lentils to a bowl and season with the salt. Scatter the chives and shallot over the lentils, then add the vinaigrette. Mix the ingredients gently to coat in the dressing before sprinkling the lardons on top.

VARIATION

There's always space for extra if you want to create a little more fanfare with this salad. Add walnuts, green apple slices, a scrape of blue cheese or a poached egg.

This salad is a classic regional-style starter found in bistros all over France. The idea of serving croutons adorned with broiled goat cheese on a bed of lettuce was popularized in the 1980s in France's goat cheese–producing regions. It's this "crunchy crouton draped in melted cheese" effect that won everyone over to make this salad a national institution. Fresh bread from the bakery and cheese from a cheese shop make a huge difference to the result. This salad is usually prepared *à la minute* (on demand) so it can be made quickly for hungry guests.

Serves 4 as a starter

1 batch dressing of your choice (page 17)

2 tbsp (30 g) unsalted butter

4 slices baguette-style bread

3.5 oz (100 g) bacon, cut into small strips (lardons)

4 handfuls mixed lettuce leaves, washed and dried

Handful of walnuts or pine nuts

4 individual small rounds of natural-rind goat cheese or a good-quality log of goat cheese, thickly sliced

MISE EN PLACE

Make the dressing according to a recipe of your choice on page 17.

In a skillet, melt the butter over medium heat and panfry the baguette slices, turning the slices over so that each side is golden brown. Panfry the bacon until crispy, then drain on a paper towel. Arrange a handful of lettuce leaves on four serving plates with a sprinkle of the bacon and nuts on top.

Just before serving, place the croutons on a baking sheet and lay a slice of goat cheese on each. Heat under the broiler for a few minutes until the cheese is lightly colored and starts to melt. Serve immediately with a drizzle of dressing over the salad and a cheesy crouton sitting on top.

CLASSIC PARISIAN SALAD

The so-called Parisian salad was born out of the burgeoning tourism trade in Paris, created from the need for cafés to offer a quick bite for foreigners near the busy train and metro stations. Today, it's part of the foodscape and a midday favorite among Parisians. All you need to re-create this Parisian icon is butter lettuce, ham, Emmentaler cheese, boiled eggs and a mustard vinaigrette.

Serves 2 as a small meal

1 batch Mustard Vinaigrette (page 17)
2 heads butter lettuce or a large bag of good-quality lettuce leaves
4 large eggs
4 slices good-quality leg ham, sliced or cut into cubes
7 oz (200 g) Emmentaler or Gruyère cheese, sliced or cut into cubes
1 tbsp (3 g) finely chopped fresh parsley or chives

MISE EN PLACE

Prepare the Mustard Vinaigrette according to the recipe on page 17. Cut the base off the lettuce and wash and dry the leaves. Trim or discard any damaged salad leaves.

Cook the eggs in boiling water for 9 minutes, then transfer to a bowl of cold water and let sit for 10 minutes before peeling and cutting them into quarters.

This salad is very much an individual affair served as a one-person serving and not a large salad to dig into. To assemble, line medium-sized plates with a bed of lettuce leaves, decorate with the ham and cheese, then lay the egg quarters neatly on top. Finish with a smattering of parsley or chives.

The mustard vinaigrette is always served in a separate bowl. It's an unspoken rule in France: Never dress a Parisian salad on behalf of another. I should also add, dressing a salad in advance will "cook" the lettuce and make it limp and droopy, so always add dressing at the last minute.

VARIATION

As some French cafés are known to do, add the following ingredients to your liking: corn kernels, tomatoes, potatoes, croutons, mushrooms or cucumber.

NIÇOISE SALAD

You need to be born in France to understand just how something as simple as a salad can spark regional conflicts. In one example from the 1900s, Auguste Escoffier dared to include potatoes in the ingredients for salade Niçoise in his seminal cooking text, *Le Guide Culinaire*. The citizens of the town of Nice were outraged that the original recipe had been meddled with. Even today, the guardians of Nice cuisine, Le Cercle de la Capelina d'Or, regard this irreverence as a sacrilege and are lobbying for the original recipe to be protected by UNESCO. Before they succeed, I took the liberty of adding green beans and a vinaigrette dressing to my recipe with the hope that the people of Nice won't take to the streets.

Serves 4 as a starter

2 batches Traditional Vinaigrette (page 17)

2 handfuls green beans

4 large eggs

3 tomatoes

2 handfuls radicchio or mixed salad leaves

½ red or green bell pepper, cut into strips, seeds and white parts discarded

½ cup (50 g) sliced celery

2 green onions (spring onion) or ½ red onion, finely sliced

7 oz (200 g) tuna in oil, flaked into small pieces

16 black olives

8 anchovy filets in oil

Handful of fresh basil, to garnish

Olive oil, to serve

MISE EN PLACE

Make the Traditional Vinaigrette according to the recipe on page 17. Double the ingredients to make two batches. Wash and dry the salad leaves. Trim or discard any damaged salad leaves.

Cook the green beans in salty boiling water for 10 minutes, then plunge into cold water and drain. Cook the eggs in boiling water for 9 minutes, then transfer to a bowl of cold water to rest for 10 minutes before peeling and cutting them in half.

While optional, it's common in French cooking to peel (*monder*) the tomatoes to improve the gustatory experience of them in salads and other dishes. To do this, use a small knife to cut an "x" on the top of each tomato and remove the stems. Boil the tomatoes whole in boiling water for 20 seconds, then immediately plunge them into a bowl of cold water. Use a small knife or your hands to peel the skin off the tomato, then cut them into quarters.

To make the salad base, arrange the green beans, salad leaves, bell peppers, celery and green onions in a large serving dish. Pour half of the dressing evenly over the salad base. Garnish the top of the salad with the tomatoes, eggs, tuna, olives and anchovy filets in whatever way pleases you. For the final touch, drizzle the rest of the dressing over the salad, decorate with basil leaves and serve with a small bowl of olive oil on the side.

NOTE

In France, this salad is more of a light meal than a starter, usually served on a plate, never in a bowl (sacrilege!). A few panfried croutons are rubbed with fresh garlic to add a tasty crunch. For the purists, the dressing is just salt, pepper and olive oil; vinegar is not welcome.

CUCUMBERS IN CREAM DRESSING

The cucumber salad is a summer classic that anyone over the age of 40 in France will have imprinted as a sweet childhood memory. But it is still on point today as a showcase of what can be done with simple, fresh ingredients that partner well together. The freshness of the herbs and tanginess of the lemon combined with the cucumbers and cream bring a dollop of summery nostalgia to your table.

Serves 4 as a starter

1 European cucumber or 2 small cucumbers

2 tbsp (30 g) coarse salt

2 tbsp (30 ml) heavy cream

½ tsp Dijon mustard

Juice of ½ lemon

1 tbsp (3 g) mixed finely chopped fresh herbs (chives, chervil or parsley), plus extra to garnish

Pinch of freshly ground pepper

Salt, to season

Pepper flakes, to garnish

1 tbsp (15 g) finely chopped green onion (spring onion), to garnish

MISE EN PLACE

Cucumbers are naturally full of water, so extract as much moisture as possible to avoid a watery dressing. To drain, peel and cut the cucumber into thin slices and layer the slices in a colander with the coarse salt sprinkled over each layer. Leave to drain over a bowl in the fridge for 1 hour, then rinse the slices under cold water and pat dry.

Combine the cream, mustard and lemon juice in a bowl. Using a whisk, whip until the mixture thickens slightly and starts to stick to the whisk, then gently stir in the herbs and pepper. Place the cucumber slices in a small salad bowl and pour the dressing over them, gently mixing it through until evenly coated. Adjust the seasoning with salt and *voilà*, your salad is ready to serve in a bowl with a smattering of mixed herbs, pepper flakes and green onion.

PARISIAN CARROT SALAD

In France, when you feel that you've had too much cream and butter, it's time to come back to crudités—and there's nothing lighter and more palate-cleansing than the Parisian carrot salad. This raw salad of finely grated carrots coated in a vinaigrette is nothing short of an institution in France, where you'll find it in cafés and restaurants and tucked away in the prepared section of supermarket aisles. I like to use a Mustard Vinaigrette (page 17) for a touch of heat, but you can use any of the Classic or Regional Vinaigrettes (page 17). Sweet carrots in season work best for this recipe.

Serves 4 as a starter

1 batch Mustard Vinaigrette (page 17)

1 lb (500 g) fresh medium-sized carrots

Pinch of salt

Pinch of freshly ground pepper

1 tbsp (3 g) finely chopped fresh parsley

Pinch of sugar (optional)

MISE EN PLACE

Prepare the Mustard Vinaigrette according to the recipe on page 17. Ensure the carrots are fridge-cold before washing and peeling them.

Grate the carrots, then place them in a large bowl. Season with the salt and pepper and stir in the parsley. If the carrots are lacking in natural sweetness, add a pinch of sugar. Just before serving, dress the carrots with the vinaigrette and toss gently. Chill in the fridge for 10 minutes before serving.

VARIATION

Some like to stir a hint of chopped garlic through the carrots. For an Asian twist, add 1 tablespoon (15 ml) of fresh orange juice, plus 1 teaspoon of finely chopped fresh cilantro.

TIP

The trick to this recipe is to grate the carrots very finely to give the salad a delicate texture. I recommend using a food processor with a fine grating blade. If doing it by hand, avoid using a coarse grating blade.

SPRING LEEKS WITH VINAIGRETTE

You may know leeks as a milder alternative to onions, used as a base for soups and stocks, but in France, this aromatic vegetable stands on its own as a light and healthy starter. We enjoy leeks that are poached to unveil a delicate soft texture and sweetness that balances well with the sharpness of a vinaigrette dressing. Packed full of vitamins and fiber, they also have a mighty reputation in France for being good for your health. This dish shines when leeks are in season and at their sweetest.

Serves 4 as a starter

1 batch Mustard Vinaigrette (page 17)
8 small spring leeks (roughly the same size)
2 tbsp (30 g) coarse salt
Handful finely chopped fresh chives or green onions (spring onion), to serve

MISE EN PLACE

Make the Mustard Vinaigrette according to the recipe on page 17. Rinse the leeks, then trim the roots and cut off the thick green leaves, keeping only the yellow-white part of the leek. Use a knife to make a small incision lengthwise along the shaft of the leek and detach three layers of outer leaves.

Gather the leeks into two bunches of four each and tie both ends with kitchen twine. Fill your largest stockpot three-quarters full of water, add the salt and bring to a boil. Boil the leeks for 20 minutes, or until tender but still holding together. Delicately scoop the leeks out of the water and drain on a paper towel. Pat them dry and transfer to a serving dish.

Spoon the vinaigrette over the leeks while they are still warm to infuse the flavor, and let them cool a little before serving. Remove the twine and dish up two leeks per person with a handful of chives or green onions.

CELERIAC SALAD WITH HOMEMADE MAYONNAISE

Celeriac (also called celery root) is often overlooked due to its unfortunate appearance. I like to think of it as the Quasimodo of the vegetable world: Underneath the rough skin lies a treasure waiting to be appreciated. Served in bistros across France, celeriac salad (*celery rémoulade*) is a simple way to discover this humble vegetable in all its glory: grated and mixed with a homemade mustard mayonnaise to reveal a moist nuttiness. Once you try it, you'll see there's no reason to be intimidated by celeriac and will appreciate it for the nutritional powerhouse that it is.

Serves 4 as a starter

1 batch Homemade Mayonnaise (page 22)

1 tbsp (15 ml) Dijon mustard

2 lemons, for prepping the celeriac

1 medium-sized celeriac

Handful of chopped fresh parsley, to garnish (optional)

Lemon slices, to garnish (optional)

MISE EN PLACE

You will need a food processor with a medium-sized grating blade to make a good celeriac rémoulade. Although you can use a hand grater, the grated celeriac pieces will be chunky and less enjoyable to eat. Make the Homemade Mayonnaise according to the recipe on page 22 and stir in the Dijon mustard.

Fill a large salad bowl with water and add the juice of one of the lemons. Cut the other lemon in half for rubbing onto the celeriac to prevent it from turning brown after peeling.

To peel the celeriac, chop off the base and top to create two flat surfaces. Rub each end with a lemon half and place on a sturdy chopping board. Grab a chef's or santoku knife and get ready to peel.

To remove the skin, firmly hold the celeriac and place the knife blade at the top so that it sits roughly at a 45-degree angle. Cut the skin, guiding the knife downward following the shape of the celeriac, to remove a thick layer of the skin. Cut like this all around the vegetable, rubbing each peeled side with lemon as you go. Once you've removed most of the skin, use a hand peeler to remove any stubborn pieces to get an even, white surface. Cut the celeriac into chunks small enough to fit into the tube of the food processor and let sit in the bowl of lemon water until you're ready to grate.

Once all the pieces are cut and you are ready to grate the celeriac, pat each piece dry and pop them into the food processor. Transfer the grated celeriac to a salad bowl, add the mayonnaise and mix until the celeriac is well coated. Serve with a sprinkle of parsley, lemon slices and a squeeze of lemon juice, if using, for extra tang.

VARIATION

Add sliced apples, grapes, walnuts and celery for an American-style Waldorf salad.

ASPARAGUS WITH MOUSSELINE SAUCE

When asparagus season begins in France, market stalls overflow with piles of green and white varieties, and this springtime dish pops up on bistro menus across the country. There's little wonder why—asparagus shines with a beautiful homemade mousseline sauce. Mousseline sauce is a light and smooth variant of hollandaise with whipped cream added to give the sauce an airy, mousse-like texture.

Serves 4 as a starter

20 green asparagus or 12 white asparagus

¾ cup (200 ml) No-Fuss Hollandaise (page 26)

1 tbsp (15 g) coarse salt

3 tbsp (45 ml) heavy cream

MISE EN PLACE

Trim the asparagus stalks, and peel the stalks if using white asparagus. About 10 minutes before you're ready to serve the asparagus, make the No-Fuss Hollandaise according to the recipe on page 26 and have the cream chilled and waiting in the fridge.

Add some salt to water in a pan and bring to a boil. Cook the asparagus in the boiling water with the salt for 5 to 10 minutes, depending on how firm or soft you like it (15 to 20 minutes for white asparagus). As soon as the asparagus is cooked, plunge them into a bowl of cold water for 1 minute to stop them from cooking further. Pat dry and transfer to a plate.

In a bowl, whip the cream until just firm and keep it chilled while you prepare the hollandaise sauce. As soon as the hollandaise is ready, gently fold the whipped cream into the sauce. Don't worry if the sauce liquefies a little; this is normal. As the sauce settles, the air in the whipped cream will produce a foamy texture. Drizzle the sauce over the asparagus and serve.

FRENCH ONION SOUP WITH PORT WINE

Onion soups date back to Roman times, but nobody is really sure who invented the version of the famous French-style onion soup that we love today. One thing we can be certain of is that this humble soup became notorious for hiding the alcohol vapor emanating from the breath of someone who had had a little too much to drink, earning it the nickname *la soupe des ivrognes* (the drunk's soup). This explains why it's common in France to enjoy a warm, cozy onion soup with friends after a boozy New Year's Eve.

Serves 4 as a starter

5 cups (1.2 L) Brown Chicken Stock (page 13) or good quality premade salt-reduced brown stock

8 slices of baguette-style bread

4 sprigs parsley

2 celery leaves

2 sprigs thyme

1 bay leaf

2 tbsp (15 g) toasted flour (see page 9)

3.5 oz (100 g) unsalted butter

1 lb (500 g) brown onions (roughly 1 onion per person), sliced

1 tbsp (15 g) sugar

1 tbsp (15 ml) port wine

1 tbsp (15 g) coarse salt

Pinch of freshly ground pepper (optional)

10.5 oz (300 g) Comté or Gruyère cheese, grated

MISE EN PLACE

If using Brown Chicken Stock, prepare in advance according to the recipe on page 13. To make the croutons, trim the slices of bread to fit the bowls used and toast them in a toaster or under the broiler. Make a bouquet garni by tying the parsley, celery leaves, thyme and bay leaf together with kitchen twine. Toast the flour according to page 9.

In a saucepan, melt the butter over medium heat and stir in the onions to evenly coat in the butter. Sprinkle in the sugar and cook for 20 minutes, or until the onions become light brown. Pour the port wine over the onions and reduce for 30 seconds, then mix in the toasted flour and stock. Season with the salt, drop in the bouquet garni and bring to a boil. Then, lower the heat to simmer the soup, partially covered, for 40 minutes, occasionally removing any foam that drifts to the surface.

Preheat your oven to broil. When the soup is ready, remove the bouquet garni and adjust the seasoning with pepper, if needed. To serve, select individual soup bowls that can hold 1 cup (250 ml) of liquid. Place one crouton at the bottom of the bowl, top with cheese, ladle in the soup and add another crouton on top. Cover with a generous amount of cheese and place under the broiler for a few minutes until the cheese is melted. Serve immediately.

CRÉCY CARROT SOUP

You will be slurping a piece of delicious history with this famous soup. The name Crécy derives from a town located in the Meaux commune, east of Paris, famous for growing the best-quality carrots in the 1900s. There, carrots were a revelation in terms of their delicate sweetness and were the star ingredient in this soup. Unfortunately, you'll most likely not find the famous Crécy carrots anywhere today, but I encourage you to hunt down the best-quality carrots you can find to make this soup.

Serves 4 as a starter

1 qt (1 L) White Chicken Stock (page 12) or good-quality premade chicken stock

9 oz (250 g) starchy potatoes

3 tbsp (45 g) unsalted butter, plus more to panfry the croutons

1 onion, finely sliced

1 lb (500 g) organic carrots, finely sliced

2 sprigs thyme

2 tsp (10 g) sugar

4 slices baguette-style bread, cut into small cubes

2–3 tbsp (30–45 ml) heavy cream or crème fraîche

Salt and pepper, to season

Handful of fresh cilantro leaves, to garnish (optional)

MISE EN PLACE

You will need an immersion blender or vegetable mill. If using White Chicken Stock, prepare in advance according to the recipe on page 12. Cut the potatoes into small cubes, placing them in a bowl of cold water.

In a medium-sized saucepan, melt the butter over low heat. As soon as the butter starts to foam, add the onion, carrots, thyme and sugar, and stir well to coat the ingredients. Cover and cook for 5 minutes.

Drain the potatoes and add them to the saucepan, mixing them in gently with the other ingredients. Pour in the stock and bring the soup to a light boil, then simmer, covered, for 15 minutes, or until the carrots and potatoes are tender.

Meanwhile, make the croutons by melting the butter and panfrying the bread cubes until golden.

When the soup is ready, turn off the heat and remove the thyme before using an immersion blender to blend the soup until lump-free and smooth. Add the cream to finish the soup and adjust the seasoning to your liking. Divide among serving bowls topped with croutons and a sprinkle of cilantro leaves (if using).

CREAMY CORN VELOUTÉ

This flavorful cream of corn soup is a tasty glimpse of how soups were made in the old days of classic French cuisine. Using a thin version of béchamel sauce as a base, this simple technique yields a soup that is rich and velvety smooth. It's a satisfying style of soup, so you don't need to serve it in large quantities. The same simple technique can be used to make a variety of soups by replacing the corn with ingredients such as mushroom and asparagus.

Serves 4 as a starter

1 oz (30 g) unsalted butter
1 oz (30 g) all-purpose flour
3¹/₃ cups (800 ml) whole milk
1 shallot, roughly chopped
1 bay leaf
1 sprig thyme
2 whole cloves
Salt and pepper, to season
2 (15-oz [400-g]) cans organic corn kernels, drained
3 tbsp (45 ml) heavy cream
1 tbsp (5 g) chopped fresh chives, to garnish

MISE EN PLACE

You'll need an immersion blender to blitz the soup velvety smooth.

To make the béchamel base, in a small saucepan, melt the butter over low heat, then add the flour all at once. Use a wooden spoon to mix the flour and butter into a paste and cook for 2 minutes. Remove from the heat and allow the roux to cool down completely.

In a separate large saucepan, combine the milk, shallot, bay leaf, thyme and cloves and season with salt and pepper. Bring to a simmer over medium-low heat, taking care not to boil the milk mixture. As soon as the milk mixture is warm, strain half of it over the cold roux sitting in the other saucepan. Turn off the heat, use a whisk to blend the milk mixture and roux together before straining the rest of the milk mixture in. Now place the saucepan over medium heat and slowly bring the milk mixture to a light boil while whisking constantly. When it starts to boil, continue to cook for 2 minutes before turning off the heat.

Immediately pour the corn kernels into the béchamel and blitz the ingredients with an immersion blender. Strain the soup through a coarse-mesh sieve into a saucepan, using a wooden spoon to press through as much of the pulp as you can. The soup should now be smooth but still on the thick side. Add the cream to adjust the consistency to your liking and correct the seasoning. Divide among small bowls and top with a sprinkle of chives.

MY SIGNATURE CHICKEN SOUP

There's nothing better than a bowl of nourishing chicken soup on a cold winter afternoon, preferably in front of a crackling log fire. I've always believed that a good chicken soup should not be complicated, and for my signature recipe, I go back to basics with a bunch of fresh garden vegetables, free-range chicken and water. The secret to a clean-tasting soup lies in the water you use. Good-quality water makes all the difference. For all my soups, I use filtered or mineral water rather than what comes out of the tap; this might seem like a fussy small thing, but it goes a long way.

Serves 4 as a starter

2 tbsp (30 g) unsalted butter

1 small leek (just the white part), finely sliced

1 onion, finely sliced

1 carrot, finely sliced

1 celery rib, finely sliced

2 cloves garlic, halved

1 bay leaf

1 sprig thyme

1 tsp cumin seeds

2 lb (1 kg) chicken thighs (on the bone)

6⅓ cups (1.5 L) filtered or mineral water

1½ tsp (8 g) coarse salt, plus more to season

½ tsp freshly ground pepper, plus more to season

1 tbsp (15 ml) olive oil

2 slices baguette-style bread, cut into cubes

¾ cup (200 ml) heavy cream

2 tbsp (6 g) chopped fresh parsley, to garnish

MISE EN PLACE

If you like your soup to be smooth, have an immersion blender ready.

In a large pot, melt the butter over medium heat, and then add the leek, onion, carrot, celery, garlic, bay leaf, thyme and cumin seeds. Gently stir the ingredients together and cook for 5 minutes. Add the chicken thighs, mixing them gently with the other ingredients, and cook for 5 minutes. Pour in the water and stir everything together once more. Finish by seasoning the soup with the coarse salt and pepper and bring the soup to a boil. When the soup starts to boil, scoop off the foam rising to the surface, then lower the heat to a light boil and set a timer for 45 minutes to cook uncovered.

Meanwhile, heat the oil and panfry the bread cubes until crisp and evenly browned. When the soup is ready, remove the chicken thighs and set aside, then discard the bay leaf and thyme. If you prefer a smooth soup, now is the time to blitz it with an immersion blender before turning off the heat.

Remove the chicken from the bones and shred with a fork, discarding the bones. Reserve a handful of the best-looking shreds for garnish and return the rest of the chicken to the soup. Stir in the cream and cook for 20 minutes over medium heat. Adjust the seasoning to your liking and serve in bowls with a sprinkle of parsley and shredded chicken. Don't forget a smattering of croutons on top.

VARIATION

For something different, add 1 teaspoon of good-quality curry powder when you add the cream. It adds a spiced edge and a wonderful yellowish tinge to the soup that I personally love.

CLASSIC SALMON TARTARE

Walk in the footsteps of the many chefs who learned how to prepare salmon tartare in French culinary school. Beautifully plated in a food ring, minced raw salmon filet is combined with an olive oil–based mayonnaise, chopped fresh herbs, capers and a touch of Tabasco for some punch. Served for brunch or as a light lunch, this small dish will make your guests feel special with its restaurant presentation. For this recipe, buy the freshest wild or farmed salmon you can find and consume it on the same day.

Serves 4 as a starter

1 lb (500 g) fresh sashimi-grade salmon filets

Fresh Herb Vinaigrette (page 17) or olive oil, for drizzling

1 large egg yolk, at room temperature

1 tsp Dijon mustard

Salt and pepper, to season

1/3 cup (80 ml) olive oil

1 tbsp (15 ml) fresh lemon juice

1/4 cup (40 g) finely chopped shallot

2 tbsp (20 g) finely chopped capers

2 tbsp (10 g) finely chopped fresh chives

2 tbsp (6 g) finely chopped fresh parsley

A few drops of Worcestershire sauce

1/2 tsp Tabasco

Paper-thin slices of cucumber or radish, to garnish

Handful of chopped fresh herbs, to garnish

Toasted baguette, to serve (optional)

NOTE

Always take the necessary safety precautions when working with raw fish.

MISE EN PLACE

You will need a food ring to plate the tartare. (I used one with a 3-inch [8-cm] diameter.) Clean the salmon filets, also removing any skin. If necessary, trim any dark pieces of flesh so you're left with the most pristine part of the filets. Keep chilled until preparation. Prepare the Fresh Herb Vinaigrette according to the recipe on page 17.

To make the flavored mayonnaise, in a medium-sized bowl, vigorously whisk the egg yolk, mustard and two pinches each of salt and pepper for 30 seconds to kick-start the emulsion. Add the olive oil a little at a time, whisking constantly, until you get a thick mayonnaise. Add the lemon juice and mix in the shallot, capers, chives and parsley. Flavor with the Worcestershire sauce and Tabasco, and add extra salt and pepper, if needed. Chill the flavored mayonnaise for 15 minutes.

Take the salmon out of the fridge and, on a clean, synthetic chopping board, use a large sharp knife to cut the filets into 1/2-inch (1.3-cm)-thick slices, followed by cutting those slices again into 1/2-inch (1.3-cm)-thick strips. Chop the strips into very small cubes. (Avoid big pieces, otherwise the tartare will fall apart when plated.)

Remove the flavored mayonnaise from the fridge and gently stir the minced salmon into it. Let it rest in the fridge for at least 10 minutes to allow the flavors to diffuse through the salmon.

To serve, position the food ring in the middle of a plate and spoon in 1/2 cup (120 g) of salmon tartare. Flatten the top with a spoon, then slowly remove the food ring to reveal a beautiful tower of tartare. Decorate the top with slices of cucumber and a sprinkle of chopped fresh herbs. Finish with a drizzle of Fresh Herb Vinaigrette or olive oil and serve with a slice of toasted baguette (optional).

BAKED EGGS À LA FLORENTINE

If you're looking for a step up from eggs Benedict for your next Sunday brunch, try these eggs à la Florentine. In France, the cooking term "à la Florentine" refers to anything cooked with spinach and Mornay sauce. Chicken, fish or vegetables . . . almost anything will work well on a bed of sautéed spinach doused in a homemade Mornay sauce and melted cheese. Broiled under the grill and served with toasted bread, this luscious, creamy egg dish will delight any spinach lover.

Serves 4 as a starter

2 cups (500 ml) Mornay sauce (page 23)

1 lb (500 g) fresh spinach leaves, washed and dried, tough stems removed

4 large eggs

Salt and pepper, to season

2 tbsp (30 g) unsalted butter

3.4 oz (100 g) grated Gruyère or Comté cheese

MISE EN PLACE

You will need four small ovenproof egg dishes to broil the eggs. Make the Mornay Sauce according to the recipe variation on page 23.

In a saucepan of boiling water, blanch the spinach with two pinches of salt: 1 minute for baby spinach and 2 minutes for mature spinach. As soon as the spinach is cooked, briefly transfer to a bowl of cold water to cool. Lightly squeeze the spinach in your hands to drain out the water, then wrap in a paper towel, giving it an extra squeeze.

Cook the eggs in boiling water for 6 minutes, then immediately settle in cold water for 5 minutes to stop them from cooking. Peel the eggs under light running water and set aside.

Season the spinach with salt and pepper and chop, then melt the butter in a skillet and sauté the spinach over high heat for 2 minutes.

To assemble the dish, have the Mornay sauce, spinach, grated cheese and eggs at the ready. Grease the dishes and spoon 3 tablespoons (40 g) of sautéed spinach onto the bottom of each dish. Use the back of a spoon to make an impression in the spinach and lay an egg into each one, then cover with a dollop of Mornay sauce and a sprinkle of cheese.

Preheat your broiler. To finish, broil under the grill for 5 minutes, or until the cheese melts and a golden crust forms on the sauce. Serve immediately with a slice of toasted bread.

MACKEREL ESCABÈCHE

In France, the word *escabèche* derives from the Catalan word *escabetx* and describes fish pickled in a vinegar-based marinade. This is an easy method to enjoy all kinds of delicate fish filets and is perfect for brunch or a light lunch. It's a dish that immediately draws the eyes to the table with its warm and summery appearance. I like to liven up the flavor even further by using two types of vinegar and a fragrant blend of aromatics. While I tend to prefer mackerel filets, any small fish, such as red mullet, will do.

Serves 4 as a starter

¼ cup (60 ml) olive oil, divided, plus extra to drizzle over the fish

1 bay leaf

1 sprig thyme

1 tsp crushed coriander seeds

1 tsp coarsely ground pepper, plus more to season

1 clove garlic, chopped finely

1 medium-sized red onion, finely sliced

1 small shallot, finely sliced

½ carrot, finely sliced

2 cups (500 ml) white wine (sauvignon blanc or Muscadet)

3 tbsp (45 ml) sherry vinegar

3 tbsp (45 ml) cider vinegar

Juice of ½ lemon

1 tsp salt, plus more to season

1 lb (500 g) mackerel filets, cleaned and trimmed

1 lemon, sliced

In a sauté pan, heat 3 tablespoons (45 ml) of oil over medium heat, then add the bay leaf, thyme, coriander, pepper and garlic. Stir gently and cook for 2 minutes, or until fragrant. Adjust the heat to low and stir in the onion, shallot and carrot, and cook for 2 minutes before adding the wine, vinegars, lemon juice and salt. Turn the heat to high to quickly bring the liquid to a boil, then simmer the marinade for 5 minutes. When done, set aside to cool while you prepare the fish.

To cook the fish, in a separate large nonstick skillet, heat the remaining olive oil over medium heat. Season the filets with salt and pepper, then place them alongside each other, skin side up, in the pan. Sear the filets for a brief 30 seconds, which is just enough time to allow the flesh to firm up. When done, gently slide the filets onto a plate.

In a ceramic baking dish, line up the fish filets, skin side up again, in a row. Pour the warm marinade over and spread the garnish evenly around the filets. Scatter the lemon slices on top and drizzle with olive oil. Cover the fish with parchment paper in direct contact with the liquid and allow to cool at room temperature before transferring to the fridge to macerate overnight. The next day, the filets should be tender, ready to be enjoyed with toasted bread, salad and a glass of wine.

CREAMY HAM AND CHEESE FEUILLETÉ

While we love puff pastry in desserts in French cooking, there are also lots of savory dishes you can make with just a couple of sheets of this buttery, flaky delicacy. One of my favorites is the *feuilleté*, which uses the technique of encasing layers of ingredients in puff pastry. For this dish, layers of ham, cheese and a creamy béchamel sauce are wrapped in dough and puffed to perfection to create one of most decadent and addictive pastry items around.

Serves 4 as a starter

1 batch Classic Béchamel Sauce (page 23), adjusted per the Mise en Place below

1–2 premade butter puff pastry sheets (depending on size)

6 or more slices good-quality ham, trimmed of excess fat

5.5 oz (150 g) grated Gruyère or Cheddar cheese

Egg wash (1 egg yolk mixed with 1 tsp water)

MISE EN PLACE

To make an extra-thick sauce for this recipe, make the Classic Béchamel recipe on page 23, but use 1.8 ounces (50 g) of butter and 1.8 ounces (50 g) of flour (instead of 1 ounce [30 grams], respectively). Refrigerate until the sauce is cold. You may need one or two sheets of pastry to make the feuilleté, depending on the size of your pastry sheets. Have the puff pastry defrosted and ready before you start. Preheat the oven to 350°F (180°C). Line a baking sheet with parchment paper.

Lay one piece of pastry on the baking sheet and keep the second sheet in the fridge for now. Arrange the slices of ham flat on the pastry without overlapping, leaving a clean 1½-inch (4-cm) margin around the edges of the pastry. Cover the ham with a thin layer of béchamel sauce, followed by a sprinkle of cheese. Repeat until you have at least three layers.

Brush around the edges of the pastry with egg wash before laying the second sheet of pastry evenly over the top. Press down firmly around the edges to seal the two pieces of pastry together, then use a knife to trim the edges. To finish, use the back of the knife to make small inward incisions along the edges, to further seal the pastry tight. Brush the top of the feuilleté generously with egg wash before chilling it in the fridge for 20 minutes.

Remove the feuilleté from the fridge, apply a second coat of egg wash and, using the back of a pointy knife, decorate the top of the feuilleté with light lines or shapes. Bake the feuilleté for 30 minutes, or until golden. Remove from the oven and rest for 10 to 15 minutes before slicing this beauty open. Serve with a salad dressed in a vinaigrette dressing, to cut through the buttery richness of the pastry.

VARIATION

Experiment with different varieties of cheese and ham to vary the flavor. For a meat-free option, replace the ham with sautéed mushrooms or roasted bell peppers.

TWICE-BAKED CHEESE AND HAM SOUFFLÉ WITH GOURMET MUSHROOMS

This is a take on an Auguste Escoffier classic that offers a glimpse of the extravagance of food service in high-end hotels and restaurants during the early 1900s. Now, I know the title sounds intimidating, but making this soufflé is easier than you think, and the ingenious twice-baked technique strips away any worry of a deflated disappointment. The gourmet mushrooms add a lovely earthy note to the cheesy cream sauce.

Makes enough for 4 soufflés

For the Mushrooms
1 oz (30 g) unsalted butter
3.5 oz (100 g) gourmet forest mushrooms
Salt and pepper, to season

For the Soufflé Base
1 oz (30 g) unsalted butter
1 oz (30 g) all-purpose flour
1 cup (250 ml) whole milk, cold
3 tbsp (45 ml) heavy cream
Salt and pepper, to season
Pinch of grated nutmeg
3 oz (80 g) grated Comté or good-quality Cheddar cheese, plus more for sprinkling
2 oz (60 g) finely chopped ham
5 large eggs, cold, separated (you will use all 5 whites but only 2 yolks)
¼ tsp fresh lemon juice

For the Cheese Sauce
1²/₃ cups (400 ml) heavy cream
Salt and pepper, to season
3 oz (80 g) grated Comté or good-quality Cheddar cheese

MISE EN PLACE
You will need four individual soufflé ramekins (approximately 4 inches [10 cm] in diameter) and a stand or hand mixer. Generously grease the ramekins, then line the bottom of each one with circles of parchment paper. Preheat the oven to 400°F (200°C). Line a baking sheet with parchment paper.

To cook the mushrooms, in a skillet, melt the butter over medium heat, then add the mushrooms with salt and pepper to season. Sauté, stirring occasionally, for 5 minutes, and then set aside.

To make the soufflé base, in a medium-sized saucepan, melt the butter over low heat and then add the flour to make a roux. Cook, stirring occasionally, for 3 minutes, or until the roux becomes a blond color. Remove from the heat and whisk in the cold milk, a little at a time, before adding the cream. Season to taste and add the nutmeg before placing the saucepan back over medium heat. Whisk constantly until the sauce thickens and starts to bubble, then stir in the cheese and the ham. When all the cheese has melted into the sauce, remove from the heat and allow to cool for a few minutes.

Once the soufflé base has cooled, stir in the 2 egg yolks, then scrape the mixture into a large bowl. Let it sit at room temperature while you prepare the egg whites.

In the bowl of a stand mixer, combine the 5 egg whites with a pinch of salt and the lemon juice and beat into a firm meringue. When ready, first whisk one-quarter of the meringue into the soufflé base to loosen it, then fold the rest in delicately with a spatula. Make sure no bits of egg white or streaks remain.

Fill each prepared ramekin three-quarters of the way full of the soufflé mixture, then transfer the ramekins to a deep baking dish. Fill the baking dish with boiling water so it reaches halfway up the sides of the ramekins. Transfer to the oven and bake for 12 minutes, or until the soufflés are well puffed and golden.

When ready, remove from the oven and allow to deflate for a few minutes before unmolding onto the baking sheet. The soufflés can be chilled in the fridge until ready to use for the second bake.

Ten minutes before serving, make the cheese sauce. In a small saucepan, heat the cream with a pinch each of salt and pepper over low heat, then stir in the cheese until fully melted.

Preheat the oven to broil on high.

For the final bake, pour just one-quarter of the cheese sauce into each serving dish, and use a spatula to carefully place each soufflé in the middle. (Don't forget to remove the parchment paper from the tops of the souffle.) Sprinkle with grated cheese. Place the dishes on a baking sheet, and broil in the oven (middle rack) for 5 minutes to crisp up the cheese and caramelize the sauce. Serve piping hot with a sprinkle of sautéed mushrooms over the cheese sauce.

MOUTHWATERING MEATS AND POULTRY

The main is the dish that everyone awaits with anticipation, so our intention here is to take the pressure off. You don't have to slave over a stove for the better part of a day to make a delicious French main, and whatever you choose here, it won't disappoint. You'll find an array of dishes catering to every occasion, from quick dishes you can whip up after a long day to more contemplative recipes for when you want to impress. This chapter explores a range of cooking methods, each with their own way of bringing flavors forward in chicken, beef, pork and lamb, including instant pan sauces, roasting, braising and tasty ragouts flavored with wine and spirits. Recipes like Braised Lamb Shanks in Port Wine (page 120) and Panfried Steak with Red Wine Sauce (page 124) will give you a good rundown of what French cooking methods are all about and how they're used in restaurants to bring that *je ne sais quoi* to a dish. Equally important for the home cook, you'll find that many recipes, like Poulet Sauté Alice (page 138) and Normandy-Style Pork Chops with Cider and Calvados Sauce (page 115) can be prepared in under an hour without sacrificing taste.

MARKET ROTISSERIE CHICKEN WITH POTATO AND TOMATO GARNISH

Returning home from the local market with a *poulet rôti* (roast chicken) is a weekend tradition for many French people. If you haven't been to a French market, the rotisserie is the stall with a line of people eyeballing racks of roasting chickens that slowly turn and drip cooking juices over a blanket of potatoes, onions and tomatoes. The chicken is always crispy with moist, tender meat and is easily devoured with the potato garnish infused with the cooking juices. This poulet rôti experience can be easily created at home using the oven.

Serves 4

For the Chicken

1 whole (3½-lb [1.6-kg]) chicken

3 tbsp (45 g) unsalted butter, at room temperature

Salt and pepper, to season

2 sprigs parsley

2 shallots, halved

2 cloves garlic, unpeeled

1 bay leaf

1 sprig thyme

2 tbsp (30 ml) cooking oil

For the Garnish

2 lb (1 kg) all-purpose potatoes (suitable for roasting)

2 tbsp (30 ml) olive oil

Salt and pepper, to season

2 onions, finely sliced

10–15 cherry tomatoes, halved

4 cloves garlic, unpeeled

1 lemon, halved and charred, to garnish (optional)

MISE EN PLACE

You will need a roasting pan large enough to comfortably fit the chicken and the potato garnish. Tie the end of the chicken legs together with kitchen twine. Peel and cut the potatoes into large cubes or quarters and let sit in a bowl of cold water. Preheat the oven to 425°F (220°C).

Pat the chicken dry on all sides before rubbing it all over with the butter. Season both inside and out with salt and pepper, then stuff the chicken with the parsley, shallots, garlic, bay leaf and thyme. Set aside.

To make the garnish, drain and pat dry the potatoes, and then place them in a bowl with the olive oil, salt and pepper, mixing everything together.

Coat the bottom of your roasting pan with the cooking oil and position the chicken on its side, then arrange the potatoes around the chicken. Transfer the pan to the oven and roast for 15 minutes on one side, then on the other side for a further 15 minutes.

After 30 minutes cooking time, remove the pan from the oven and position the chicken on its back (belly side up). Stir the onions in with the potatoes to coat well in oil, then add the tomatoes and the garlic. Return the pan to the oven. Lower the heat to 350°F (180°C) and roast for 45 minutes, or until the chicken is golden and cooked through.

Transfer the chicken to a plate, but leave the potato garnish in the oven to crisp up while the chicken is resting. Cover the chicken with foil and let rest for at least 15 minutes before carving. Serve the chicken in a large dish surrounded by the garnish.

TIP

The roasting time for chicken is based on weight. As a rough guide, count 25 minutes per 1 pound (500 g) of meat. A resting time of at least 15 minutes is crucial to ensure the meat is moist and juicy. To test that the chicken is cooked through, probe the thigh with a food thermometer. The chicken is done when the internal temperature of the thigh is at least 165°F (74°C).

BISTRO STEAK AND FRIES WITH HERB BUTTER

Settle in for the quintessential bistro experience: grilled prime cut of beef (rib eye or sirloin) delicately sliced and served with Steak Herb Butter (page 21) and crispy homemade fries. A crunchy salad dressed in a Mustard Vinaigrette (page 17) adds freshness to the plate and comes in handy to mop up the little pools of melted butter.

Serves 2

6 slices Steak Herb Butter (page 21)

1 batch Mustard Vinaigrette (page 17)

1 lb (500 g) starchy potatoes, scrubbed

Salt and pepper, to season

2 (9-oz [250-g] and 1½" [4-cm]-thick) rib eye or sirloin steaks

2 handfuls lettuce leaves (I like to use butter lettuce)

MISE EN PLACE

Prepare a deep fryer with 2 to 3 quarts (2 to 3 L) of cooking oil, depending on the size of the deep fryer, to cook the fries. Make the Steak Herb Butter in advance according to the recipe on page 21 and ensure it's fridge cold (not frozen). Prepare the Mustard Vinaigrette according to the recipe on page 17. Cut the potatoes into thin fries, then immerse in a bowl of cold water. Preheat the oven to 120°F (50°C).

To precook the fries, bring the temperature of the deep fryer oil to 320°F (160°C). Drain and pat the potatoes dry before placing them in the fryer basket, carefully lowering it into the hot oil. Cook for 4 to 5 minutes, then remove the basket and let it sit to drain. Increase the temperature to 375°F (190°C) in preparation for the second cooking.

Season the steaks and grill or panfry until medium rare, or when the internal temperature reaches 135°F (57°C). Transfer to a plate, cover and keep warm in the oven along with the serving plates.

Now, lower the fries back into the oil to cook a second time for 4 to 5 minutes, or until crisp and golden. Sit the fries on a paper towel–lined plate to drain before transferring them to a serving bowl and seasoning with salt.

In a salad bowl, combine the lettuce and the Mustard Vinaigrette and toss until the lettuce is well coated and shiny. Serve the steaks on the warm plates with two or three slices of the herb butter melting on top and the salad and fries on the side.

TIP

When frying a large quantity of fries, cook in batches not exceeding 1 pound (500 g), for best results.

MAÎTRE D' STEAK TARTARE

It's fair to say that the world has a love-hate relationship with steak tartare, but for the lovers out there, and the curious, this delicate starter is a delight thanks to its succulent texture and punchy flavor. It was always a small thrill to order a steak tartare in France, where it is traditionally prepared by the headwaiter in front of you, but now you can do this yourself at home.

Serves 4

10.5 oz (300 g) prime beef filet

1 large egg yolk

1 tsp Dijon mustard

5 tbsp (75 ml) olive oil

1 tbsp (10 g) finely diced shallot

1 tbsp (3 g) chopped fresh parsley

2 tsp (3 g) chopped fresh chives

2 tsp (5 g) chopped capers

2 tsp (5 g) chopped gherkins, plus sliced gherkins, to garnish

1 tsp ketchup

Few drops of Tabasco

Few drops of Worcestershire sauce

Salt and pepper, to season

1 tbsp (3 g) fresh herbs, to garnish

MISE EN PLACE

You will need a 3-inch (8-cm) or smaller food ring to plate the steak tartare. Cut the beef filet into small cubes, then process for a few seconds in a food processor, using the pulse function. Transfer to a container and keep chilled tightly sealed in the fridge.

In a large bowl, mix the egg yolk and mustard together, then slowly stir in the olive oil with a fork. Add the shallot, parsley, chives, capers, gherkins and ketchup and mix together with a spoon. Tap a few drops of Tabasco and Worcestershire sauce into the mixture and season.

Remove the meat from the fridge and gently mix it into the dressing, a little at a time. Your steak tartare is almost ready. Before serving, keep the tartare chilled, covered, in the fridge for 10 minutes to allow the flavors to infuse. Use the food ring to plate the tartare, then garnish with fresh herbs, gherkins and a grind of pepper. Some toasted bread on the side will seal the deal.

NOTE

I must stress, it's crucial that you use the freshest and best-quality prime cut of meat you can buy and use it on the same day. The meat must also be fridge cold before starting.

SEARED CHICKEN BREASTS IN CREAMY MUSHROOM SAUCE

This dish makes the most of the succulent juices rendered from a chicken breast, blending them with cream, white wine and mushrooms. The result is a silky sauce that can be made on a whim without using stock, which is a real time-saver. The wine can be easily replaced with port or Madeira wine, so you can use whatever you have on hand. The same goes for the meat: Any white meat, such as pork or veal, will work for this recipe. This is one of my go-to "lazy but tasty" recipes.

Serves 4

For the Chicken
4 chicken breasts, skin off
Salt and pepper, to season
2 tbsp (30 g) unsalted butter
1 tbsp (15 ml) cooking oil

For the Sautéed Mushrooms
2 tbsp (30 ml) olive oil
9 oz (250 g) button mushrooms, sliced thinly

For the Sauce
4 tbsp (40 g) finely diced shallot
3 tbsp (45 ml) white wine
¾ cup (200 ml) heavy cream
Salt and pepper, to season
1 tbsp (3 g) chopped fresh parsley, to garnish

MISE EN PLACE
Trim any excess fat off the chicken, then lightly score the underside of each breast and season with salt and pepper. Preheat the oven to 120°F (50°C).

In a large skillet, heat the olive oil, and panfry the mushrooms over medium heat for 5 minutes, or until golden. Set aside.

In a large stainless-steel skillet, melt and heat the butter and cooking oil, over medium heat, and sear the chicken breasts for 5 minutes on each side, or until golden. When both sides are seared, continue to cook, turning the chicken regularly until cooked through. (The internal temperature should be 165°F [74°C].) Cooking the meat gently over moderate heat like this will caramelize plenty of the juices for the sauce. Transfer the chicken to a plate, cover with foil and keep warm in the oven while you make the sauce.

To make the sauce, add the shallot to the same skillet used to cook the chicken. Cook over low heat, stirring occasionally, for 2 minutes, and then moisten with the wine and detach the caramelized juices sticking to the bottom of the pan with a wooden spoon. Increase the heat to high and reduce until roughly 1 tablespoon (15 ml) of wine remains. Add the cream and sautéed mushrooms, mixing well, and then lower the heat to medium and simmer for 5 minutes, or until the sauce is thick enough to coat the back of a spoon.

Return the chicken and any accumulated juices back to the pan. Baste the chicken with the sauce for 2 minutes and season to taste. Serve the chicken drenched in the sauce with a sprinkle of parsley and a side of greens.

BEEF DAUBE WITH SPRING CARROTS

This one-pot recipe is an old family classic that has unfortunately slipped into the shadow of *bœuf bourguignon* in recent times. But it deserves to be resurrected. *Bœuf carottes* (also known as beef daube) uses a similar technique to bœuf bourguignon, except that the meat is cooked in white wine instead of red. The abundance of carrots also counterbalances the acidity of the white wine to give the sauce a distinctive sweet and floral character. With few ingredients and no need for a stock, this is a great recipe for a lazy Sunday family dinner.

Serves 4–6

2 lb (1 kg) chuck or shoulder roast

Salt and pepper, to season

2 tbsp (15 g) toasted flour (see page 9)

2 tbsp (30 ml) cooking oil

3.5 oz (100 g) smoked bacon, cut into thick strips (lardons)

10 pearl onions or 5 small shallots

1 sprig thyme

1 bay leaf

1 tsp peppercorns

5 juniper berries

2 cups (500 ml) dry white wine (French sauvignon blanc)

3 tbsp (45 ml) cognac

1/3 cup (80 ml) water, plus more as needed

1 lb (500 g) spring carrots, cut into large batons

MISE EN PLACE

You will need a Dutch oven or a cast-iron pot. Let the meat sit at room temperature for 20 minutes before cooking. Cut into large cubes and season with salt and pepper. Toast the flour according to page 9.

In the Dutch oven, heat the oil over medium-high heat and sear the meat on all sides until dark brown, then transfer to a plate. Using the same pot, sauté the bacon and onions over medium heat, stirring constantly, for 3 minutes, or until lightly browned. Scrape the mixture into a bowl and set aside.

Return the meat to the pot along with the thyme, bay leaf, peppercorns and juniper berries, then stir in the toasted flour. Now, pour in the wine and cognac, and top with enough water so that the combined liquid barely covers the meat. Bring to a boil and scoop off any foam floating to the surface, then simmer, uncovered, for 1 hour.

Add the carrots along with the sautéed onions and bacon. Cover and simmer for 1½ to 2 hours, or until the meat is cooked through and comes apart easily when prodded with a fork. Transfer the meat to a serving dish and carefully arrange the vegetable garnish around it. To finish, reduce the sauce over high heat for 3 to 4 minutes, then pour it over the meat. I love this dish with mashed potatoes or French-Style Pilaf Rice (page 161).

NORMANDY-STYLE PORK CHOPS
WITH CIDER AND CALVADOS SAUCE

Normandy is known for its no-fuss dishes, and this recipe, made in 30 minutes, is no exception. The chops are sautéed and served with a pan sauce flavored with hard apple cider and Calvados. The garnish is also made of apples that are sautéed in butter, creating a finely balanced sweet and savory flavor that dances on the palate. There's no stock to build the sauce in this recipe, so it's important to cook the chops slowly over moderate heat to produce lots of caramelized meat juices, which give deep color and flavor to the sauce.

Serves 4

For the Apple Garnish
2 apples (Golden Delicious or similar)
Juice from ½ lemon
2 tbsp (30 g) unsalted butter
Salt and pepper, to season
1 stem scallions, chopped, for garnish (optional)

For the Chops
4 pork chops or cutlets
Salt and pepper, to season
2 tbsp (30 g) unsalted butter
1 tbsp (15 ml) cooking oil

For the Sauce
½ cup (120 ml) hard apple cider
½ cup (120 ml) heavy cream
1–2 tsp (5–10 ml) Calvados

MISE EN PLACE
Peel and core the apples and place the apples in a bowl of water mixed with the lemon juice to prevent them from turning brown. Preheat the oven to 120°F (50°C) and season the pork chops with salt and pepper.

To cook the chops, in a large skillet, heat the butter and oil over medium heat. When the butter foams, add the seasoned chops and sear for 5 minutes on each side, or until golden brown. Once both sides are seared, continue to cook until the internal temperature of the chops reaches around 150°F (65°C), then transfer to a baking sheet, cover with foil and keep warm in the oven.

To make the apple garnish, rinse and finely slice the apples. In a nonstick frying pan, melt the butter and sauté the apples for 10 minutes. Season with salt and pepper. Once the apples are golden brown, set aside.

To make the sauce, remove any excess fat from the pan used to cook the chops. Over high heat, pour in the cider, and use a wooden spoon to blend the caramelized juices on the bottom of the pan with the cider to create the base of the sauce. Reduce for 2 minutes, add the cream, then reduce again for at least 3 minutes, or until the sauce is thick enough to coat the back of a spoon. Turn the heat to low, adjust the seasoning to your taste and add the Calvados.

Return the pork chops and any accumulated juices to the pan and simmer in the sauce for 3 minutes before serving. Serve the chops in a pool of sauce with the apple garnish on top and some chopped scallions, if using. For the true Normandy experience, enjoy with a glass of hard apple cider.

STEAK AU POIVRE

Steak au Poivre is so iconic it almost needs no introduction, but there are so many versions of this recipe that it's hard to pin down the best one. After having tried many pepper steak sauces over the years, my favorite recipe uses a combination of stock, wine and cognac with a little time for the steak to infuse with the freshly crushed peppercorns. And speaking of peppercorns, try getting your hands on a single-origin pepper to up the flavor ante, such as the long pepper from Java, Indonesia. You'll thank me later.

Serves 2

For the Steak

2 tbsp (13 g) coarsely crushed black or mixed peppercorns

2 prime steaks (sirloin, filet or rib eye)

1 tbsp (15 ml) cooking oil

1 tbsp (15 g) unsalted butter

For the Sauce

⅔ cup (150 ml) Homestyle Demi-Glace (page 15)

1 small shallot, finely diced

3 tbsp (45 ml) white wine

4 tbsp (60 ml) heavy cream

1 tbsp (15 ml) cognac

MISE EN PLACE

Use a spice grinder or mortar and pestle to coarsely grind the peppercorns. Make the Homestyle Demi-Glace in advance according to the recipe on page 15. Preheat the oven to 120°F (50°C).

Evenly coat the surface of the steaks with the ground peppercorns, using your hands to apply some pressure on the surface so they stick to the meat. Let sit for at least 15 minutes to allow the pepper flavor to diffuse through the meat.

In a stainless-steel skillet or sauté pan, heat the oil and butter over medium heat, then sear the steaks, turning them over just once while cooking. Don't flash sear them for this recipe, but cook slowly over moderate heat to allow the meat juices to caramelize without burning the pepper. (Burning the peppercorns will create an unpleasant bitterness in the sauce.)

Cook the steak to your desired level of doneness; I recommend medium rare or an internal temperature of 135°F (57°C). When done, transfer to a plate, cover with foil and keep warm in the oven while you make the sauce.

To make the sauce, using the same pan, sauté the shallot over low heat for 1 minute, then pour in the wine and use a spoon to detach the brown bits stuck to the bottom of the pan. Increase the heat to high and reduce until roughly 2 teaspoons (10 ml) of liquid remains, then add the demi-glace and let it reduce by half. Mix in the cream and continue to reduce for 3 minutes, or until the sauce is thick enough to coat the back of a spoon. To finish, adjust the heat to low, mix in the cognac, then return the steaks with their accumulated juices back to the pan. Simmer the steaks in the sauce for 2 minutes before serving.

CHICKEN CHASSEUR

Legend has it that in medieval times, the small game from the hunting parties of noblemen was cast off to the house cook, who would turn it into a hearty meal with foraged mushrooms and herbs. Known and loved today as the famous hunter's chicken, this dish is prepared using sautéed chicken cooked in a fragrant sauce of tomato-flavored stock, cognac, mushrooms and white wine, finished with fresh tarragon. It's a must to use the Homestyle Demi-Glace (page 15) for this dish to really shine.

Serves 4–6

For the Chicken

2 lb (1 kg) chicken pieces (breast, thighs and legs)

Salt and pepper, to season

1 tbsp (8 g) all-purpose flour

1 tbsp (15 ml) cooking oil

For the Sauce

1¼ cups (300 ml) Homestyle Demi-Glace (page 15)

7 oz (200 g) button mushrooms, quartered

3 tbsp (30 g) finely diced shallot

1 tbsp (15 ml) tomato paste

2 tbsp (30 ml) cognac, plus a dash to finish the sauce

⅓ cup (80 ml) white wine

2 tbsp (10 g) chopped fresh tarragon, plus more to garnish

1 tbsp (3 g) chopped fresh parsley, plus more to garnish

2 tbsp (30 g) unsalted butter, to finish the sauce (optional)

MISE EN PLACE

You will need a Dutch oven or cast-iron pot. Season the chicken pieces with salt and pepper and dust them with the flour. Preheat the oven to 400°F (200°C). Make the Homestyle Demi-Glace in advance according to the recipe on page 15.

To make the chicken, in the pot, heat the oil over medium-high heat until it sizzles. First, sear the chicken on each side for 5 minutes, then cover the pot and transfer to the oven to cook for 25 to 30 minutes, or until the internal temperature of the meat reaches 165°F (74°C). The chicken breasts will cook faster, so remove them after 15 minutes. When cooked, transfer the chicken to a plate and let stand, covered, while you make the sauce.

To make the sauce, place the same pot over medium heat and sauté the mushrooms for 3 minutes, or until golden. Add the shallot and tomato paste and cook for 1 minute to allow the flavor to develop. Stir in the cognac and wine, then scrape the bottom of the pan gently with a wooden spoon to detach the caramelized juices. Let the liquid reduce until roughly 1 tablespoon (15 ml) remains, then add the demi-glace and reduce again for 5 minutes or more, until the sauce is thick enough to coat the back of a spoon. Lower the heat, stir in the tarragon and parsley and adjust the seasoning to your liking.

To finish, return the chicken and any accumulated juices back to the pot and simmer for 5 to 10 minutes, or until the chicken is warm enough to serve. For an extra boost of flavor, stir in the butter with a dash of cognac and garnish with the herbs.

BRAISED LAMB SHANKS IN PORT WINE

My favorite way to prepare lamb shanks is braised until the meat is tender and falling off the bone. Braising is a simple cooking method that involves slow cooking meat partly submerged in stock and wine. By the time the meat is cooked, the stock has reduced and transformed into a delicious sauce. Using wine is the standard, but sometimes I like to use fortified port for an intensely rich and deep sauce that makes you feel like you're sitting down to a restaurant meal without having to leave the house.

Serves 2–4

2 cups (500 ml) Brown Chicken Stock (page 13) or good-quality premade beef or veal stock

2 lamb shanks

Salt and pepper, to season

2 tbsp (30 ml) cooking oil

1 carrot, roughly chopped

1 white onion, roughly chopped

1 shallot, roughly chopped

2 cloves garlic

1 bay leaf

2 small sprigs rosemary

1 tsp tomato paste

½ cup (120 ml) ruby port wine, plus a dash to finish the sauce (optional)

1 tbsp (15 g) unsalted butter

MISE EN PLACE

You will need a large Dutch oven or cast-iron pot. If using, make the Brown Chicken Stock in advance according to the recipe on page 13. Bring the stock to a light boil and set aside. Preheat the oven to 325°F (165°C) and season the lamb shanks with salt and pepper.

In the Dutch oven, heat the oil, then sear the shanks on all sides until crusty and brown. Transfer them to a plate and set aside.

Add the carrot, onion, shallot, garlic, bay leaf and rosemary to the Dutch oven and cook for 2 minutes, or until fragrant, and then stir in the tomato paste. Pour in the port wine and cook for 2 minutes before returning the shanks to the pot. Top with the stock, no higher than halfway up to the meat. (You don't want to submerge the shanks in liquid.) Bring the liquid to a simmer, then transfer the pot to the oven and braise for between 2½ to 3 hours, or until the meat falls apart easily when prodded with a fork. Once cooked, transfer the meat to a plate and cover while you make the sauce.

Place the pot back on the stove over high heat to reduce the remaining liquid for 10 minutes, then strain the sauce through a sieve into a saucepan. To finish, place the saucepan over medium heat and add a dash of port wine, if you wish. When the sauce starts to simmer, turn off the heat and stir in the butter to bind the sauce.

Serve the shanks on a plate in a pool of sauce. There's no better combination than pairing the braised lamb shanks with creamy mashed potatoes to soak up the rich sauce.

BRAISED CHICKEN IN TARRAGON SAUCE

With its subtle anise notes, tarragon is one of the most underrated herbs for cooking, which is why I can't resist a dish where this distinctive herb is the hero. This recipe uses both the stalks and the tarragon leaves to break through the creamy sauce with its licorice accent. This is such a crowd-pleaser and one of the most popular dishes in the French Cooking Academy's back catalog. Hopefully, it becomes part of your monthly meat rotation at home.

Serves 4

¾ cup (200 ml) Brown Chicken Stock (page 13) or good-quality premade brown stock

1 bunch fresh tarragon (stalks and leaves)

6 chicken pieces of your choice (thighs, breast or legs)

Salt and pepper, to season

2 tbsp (15 g) flour

1 tbsp (15 ml) cooking oil

1 carrot, roughly diced

1 shallot, roughly diced

1 celery rib, finely sliced

2 tbsp (30 g) unsalted butter

3 tbsp (45 ml) cognac

¾ cup (200 ml) dry white wine

¾ cup (200 ml) heavy cream

MISE EN PLACE

You will need a Dutch oven or cast-iron pot. If using, make the Brown Chicken Stock in advance according to the recipe on page 13. Bring the stock to a light boil and set aside. Strip and reserve the leaves from the tarragon and tie the stalks into a bunch with kitchen twine. Season the chicken with salt and pepper and dust lightly with the flour.

In the Dutch oven, heat the oil over medium-high heat and sear the chicken pieces for 5 minutes on each side, until golden brown (cooking in batches, if needed). When cooked, transfer the chicken to a plate and set aside, covered.

Lower the heat to medium, add the carrot, shallot, celery and butter, and cook for 1 minute, stirring well to avoid burning the ingredients. Pour in the cognac and scrape the bottom of the pan to detach the caramelized juices before stirring in the wine. Reduce until roughly 2 tablespoons (30 ml) of liquid remain.

Slide the chicken back into the pot, along with any residual cooking juices, and adjust the heat to low. Bury the bunch of tarragon stalks under the chicken and pour in the stock along with a pinch of salt and pepper. Simmer, covered, for 35 minutes. Remove the chicken breasts after 15 minutes of cooking and set aside covered with foil. After 35 minutes, discard the tarragon stalks and scoop out the rest of the chicken to sit with the resting chicken breasts.

To make the sauce, add the cream to the pot and bring to a boil over high heat, then lower the heat slightly and let the sauce bubble away for 5 to 10 minutes, or until the consistency thickens enough to coat the back of the spoon.

Adjust the heat to low, and stir in a small handful of the tarragon leaves. Return the chicken to the pot, gently turning the pieces to coat in the sauce. Simmer, covered, for 5 minutes before serving divided among dinner plates with a generous ladleful of sauce and a pinch of extra tarragon leaves.

PANFRIED STEAK WITH RED WINE SAUCE

To make the vibrant red wine sauce for this recipe, the pan sauce technique uses the meat juices produced from cooking the meat blended with a good-quality wine. In France, we live by the maxim "cook with wine that you want to drink." Now, I'm not saying you need to secure a Bordeaux premier cru to make this recipe, but avoid the bottom-shelf wine selection. Not only will this make the sauce shine, but you will also appreciate a sip or two while cooking. For the meat, rib eye is the way to go.

Serves 2

For the Steaks
2 prime steaks, preferably rib eye

Salt and freshly ground pepper, to season

1 tbsp (15 ml) cooking oil

For the Sauce
¼ cup (60 g) unsalted butter, cut into small cubes, divided

2 shallots, finely chopped

½ cup (120 ml) good-quality red wine

1 clove garlic, bruised

1 sprig thyme

1 small bay leaf

½ tsp Dijon mustard

2 tbsp (6 g) finely chopped fresh curly parsley, to garnish

MISE EN PLACE
Season the steaks with salt and pepper and let sit at room temperature for 20 minutes before cooking. Preheat the oven to 120°F (50°C).

In a medium-sized stainless-steel skillet or sauté pan, heat the oil over high heat, and sear the steaks. Cook to your desired level of doneness (ideally medium rare), flipping the steak several times in the pan to cook evenly on both sides (this also helps produce lots of caramelized juices at the bottom of the pan). When cooked, transfer the steaks to a plate, cover with foil and keep warm in the oven while you make the sauce.

To make the sauce, remove any oil from the pan, melt 1 tablespoon (15 g) of the butter over medium heat then cook the shallots for 1 minute. Add the wine, garlic, thyme and bay leaf, then increase the heat to high and reduce until roughly ¼ cup (60 ml) of liquid remains and the sauce becomes syrupy. Turn off the heat and whisk in the remaining butter, followed by the mustard. To finish, pour the accumulated juices from the steak into the sauce and adjust the seasoning to your liking. Strain the sauce before serving drizzled over the steak and garnish with the parsley.

BEAUJOLAIS-STYLE CHICKEN

Beaujolais chicken is like the classic coq au vin but prepared the easy way. This one-pot recipe requires only a good-quality chicken, some vegetables, aromatics and a good dose of red wine. A note about the wine: Pinot noir goes just as well as a Beaujolais.

Serves 4–6

1¼ cups (300 ml) Brown Chicken Stock (page 13) or good-quality premade chicken stock

1 whole (3½-lb [1½-kg]) chicken, cut into 4–6 pieces

Salt and pepper, to season

1 tbsp (8 g) all-purpose flour

2 tbsp (15 g) toasted flour (see page 9)

2 tbsp (30 ml) cooking oil

1 clove garlic, halved

5.5 oz (150 g) smoked bacon, cut into large strips (lardons)

1 shallot, cut into medium-sized cubes

1 onion, cut into medium-sized cubes

2 carrots, sliced

1 bay leaf

1 sprig thyme

1 bottle medium-bodied red wine

2 tbsp (30 g) unsalted butter

7 oz (200 g) button mushrooms, quartered

1 clove garlic, finely chopped

2 tbsp (6 g) finely chopped fresh parsley

MISE EN PLACE

You will need a Dutch oven or cast-iron pot. If using, make the Brown Chicken Stock ahead according to the recipe on page 13. Bring the stock to a light boil and set aside. Season the chicken pieces with salt and pepper and dust with the flour. Toast 2 tablespoons (15 g) of flour according to page 9.

In the pot, heat the oil over medium heat and evenly sear the chicken until golden-brown (cooking in batches, if needed). Remove the chicken from the pot and set aside.

Using the same pot, add the garlic, bacon, shallot, onion, carrots, bay leaf and thyme and cook, stirring occasionally, for 3 minutes, or until lightly seared. Now add the chicken back in and sprinkle with the toasted flour. Stir to combine with the other ingredients and cook for 2 minutes.

To add the wine, first pour in roughly ½ cup (120 ml), scraping the bottom of the pan with a wooden spoon to detach the caramelized juices, before adding the rest. Now incorporate the stock and bring to a boil. Lower the heat to medium-low and remove any foam floating on the surface. Simmer, uncovered, for 45 to 50 minutes, or until the chicken is cooked through. After 20 minutes of cooking, remove the chicken breasts and set aside covered with foil.

Meanwhile, in a small skillet, melt the butter and sauté the mushrooms over high heat until golden (about 5 minutes).

When the chicken is cooked, ladle it into a dish and discard the bay leaf and thyme. Leave the rest of the cooking liquid in the pot.

To make the sauce, bring the cooking liquid to a boil and reduce for at least 10 minutes, until the sauce becomes thick enough to coat the back of a spoon. Adjust the heat to low and place the chicken and any accumulated juices back into the pot along with the mushrooms, garlic and parsley. Mix gently and simmer for 3 minutes to make sure the chicken is warm enough to serve. Arrange the chicken pieces on a serving dish and cover with the sauce.

BAKED LAMB CHOPS "CHAMPVALLON"
WITH ONIONS AND POTATOES

There's an interesting legend behind this dish that predates the fierce competition of today's *MasterChef*. The mistresses of King Louis XIV, Madame Champvallon and the king's favorite, Madame de Maintenon, battled it out to win the king's favor with food. Now, the very ambitious Madame Champvallon attempted to steal away the king's attention with this dish of seared lamb chops on a bed of caramelized onions bathed in a lamb jus and baked in a blanket of finely sliced crispy potatoes. (This dish is so delicious, I'm sure it worked for a little while, at least.)

Serves 4

¾ cup (200 ml) White Chicken Stock (page 12) or good-quality premade chicken stock, divided

5 fresh parsley stalks

1 bay leaf

1 sprig thyme

4 lamb chops (rib, loin or shoulder)

Salt and pepper, to season

1 lb (500 g) yellow waxy potatoes

3 tbsp (45 ml) olive oil, divided

2 tbsp (30 g) unsalted butter

2 onions, sliced

1 clove garlic, bruised

MISE EN PLACE

You will need a medium-sized baking dish. If using, make the White Chicken Stock in advance according to the recipe on page 12. Bring the stock to a light boil and set aside. To make a bouquet garni, tie the parsley stalks, bay leaf and thyme together with kitchen twine. Trim any excess fat off the chops and season. Preheat the oven to 425°F (220°). Use a mandoline to finely slice the potatoes ¼-inch (6-mm) thick, then immerse in cold water.

In a large stainless-steel skillet or sauté pan, heat 1 tablespoon (15 ml) of the oil over medium heat, then sear the chops on each side for 3 minutes, or until light brown. Transfer the chops to rest on a plate.

Using the same pan over medium heat, melt the butter, then stir in the onions and season. Cook, stirring occasionally, for 10 minutes, or until soft and semi-caramelized. Remove from the heat and set aside.

Drain and pat dry the potato slices, then toss them in a bowl with the remaining oil and some seasoning. In the same pan, cook the potatoes for 3 minutes over medium heat, then add 3 tablespoons (45 ml) of the stock and swirl the pan to blend in the caramelized juices gathered on the bottom. Let the potatoes cook until most of the liquid has evaporated, then turn off the heat.

Lightly oil the baking dish and neatly arrange the chops without overlapping. Cover the chops with the onions and lodge the bouquet garni and garlic between the chops. Pour the remaining stock into the dish, then lay the potato slices on top and season. Bake for 40 minutes, or until the potatoes are crisp and light brown.

Serve the chops piping hot with a generous spoonful of onion garnish and lamb jus. Serve with Lyonnaise Sautéed Green Beans (page 162).

PORK CHOPS WITH MUSTARD AND GHERKIN SAUCE

I am not surprised that this Parisian classic has stood the test of time. Spooned over perfectly seared pork chops, there's something about the tangy combination of wine, mustard and gherkins that tickles the taste buds. It's exactly the kind of comfort dish you would expect to be served in a small Parisian bistro with a side of sautéed potatoes and a glass of wine. In just 30 minutes or so, you can be serving this dish at the table, and be transported back to the City of Love.

Serves 2

For the Sauce
⅔ cup (150 ml) Homestyle Demi-Glace (page 15)
1 tbsp (15 g) butter
½ onion, finely chopped
3 tbsp (45 ml) dry white wine
2 tsp (10 ml) strong Dijon mustard
2 tbsp (20 g) finely sliced gherkins
Salt and freshly ground pepper, to season

For the Chops
1 tbsp (15 ml) cooking oil
1 tbsp (15 g) butter
2 pork chops, trimmed of excess fat

MISE EN PLACE
Make the Homestyle Demi-Glace in advance according to the recipe on page 15. Preheat the oven to 120°F (50°C).

To cook the chops, in a large skillet, heat the oil and butter over medium heat and sear the chops on each side until golden with an internal temperature of 150°F (65°C) (about 15 minutes in total). Transfer the chops to a plate and rest, covered, in the oven while you make the sauce.

To make the sauce, remove the excess fat from the same skillet, then melt the butter over low heat and sauté the onion for 10 minutes. Add the wine and use a wooden spoon to detach those deliciously crispy bits of caramelized juices, then reduce until roughly ½ tablespoon (8 ml) of liquid remains. Increase the heat to high, add the demi-glace and boil for 3 minutes, or until the sauce becomes thick enough to coat the back of a spoon. Turn off the heat, gently stir in the mustard and gherkins and adjust the seasoning to your liking.

There are two ways to serve this classic dish. The first option is to turn the seared chops in the sauce to fully coat them, serving straight from the pan. The second is to serve on warm plates with a drizzle of sauce, leaving the rest in a small serving dish for guests to help themselves.

SLOW-COOKED BEEF IN DARK BELGIAN BEER

This popular dish, enjoyed in northeast France, originated in Belgium. For our northern colleagues, it's their answer to bœuf bourguignon, whereby the red wine is replaced by a dark Belgian beer. Like beef bourguignon, the dish is slow-cooked, but the flavor is drastically different with the dark beer lending a malty sweetness to the beef. For the Belgian beer, I like to use a Chimay Blue Grande Réserve, which is rich with malty caramel notes, but feel free to experiment with other varieties.

Serves 4

2-lb (1-kg) piece of beef chuck (or other cuts suited for slow cooking), cut into ¾" (2-cm)-thick slices

Salt and pepper, to season

1 tbsp (8 g) toasted flour (see page 9)

1 tbsp (15 ml) cooking oil

1 tbsp (15 g) unsalted butter

4 onions, finely sliced

5 tbsp (15 g) finely chopped fresh mixed herbs (parsley, chives, tarragon or chervil), plus more to garnish

1 tbsp (15 ml) vinegar

1 tbsp (15 g) dark brown sugar

1 bay leaf

Few sprigs thyme

13.5-fl oz (400-ml) Belgian dark beer (I use Chimay Blue Grande Réserve)

2 tbsp (20 g) chopped capers, to garnish

MISE EN PLACE

You will need a Dutch oven or cast-iron pot. Preheat the oven to 300°F (150°C) and season the meat with salt and pepper. Toast the flour according to page 9.

In the pot, heat the oil over high heat and sear the meat in batches until browned on both sides. When done, transfer to a plate and set aside.

Using the same pot, melt the butter and sauté the onions over medium heat for at least 15 minutes, stirring often, until light brown and slightly caramelized. Stir in the toasted flour and cook for 2 minutes before scraping the onions into a bowl.

Layer the ingredients into the pot, starting with some meat slices, onions and a sprinkling of fresh herbs. Repeat layering the ingredients in this order until nothing is left. When done, pour in the vinegar, along with the brown sugar, bay leaf and thyme. Season with a few pinches of salt and pepper. Pour the beer into the pot, pop on the lid and cook in the oven for 3 hours, or until the meat is tender and can be easily pulled apart with a fork. After 2 hours' cooking, check whether the liquid has reduced by more than half. If so, top up with a little water.

When the meat is tender and succulent, remove the bay leaf and thyme and get ready to serve. Divide the meat among dinner plates and serve drizzled with the sauce and a sprinkle of herbs and capers. Pair with homemade French fries and a glass of the tasty beer used for cooking.

BRAISED CHICKEN THE CORSICAN WAY

The island of Corsica, where Napoleon was born, really should be on your bucket list of places to visit. Located in the Mediterranean Sea, just west of Italy, it's one of the most scenic and beautiful parts of France. The food culture in Corsica has evolved into a distinctive cuisine, and this recipe is an example of its French and Italian influences. The chicken is cooked the Corsican way, seared whole before being braised with a marriage of Franco-Italian ingredients: tomatoes, green olives, Italian-style cured ham, garlic, red wine and cognac (Napoleon's favorite drink).

Serves 4

¾ cup (200 ml) Brown Chicken Stock (page 13) or good-quality premade brown stock

1 whole (3½-lb [1½-kg]) chicken

Salt and pepper, to season

1 tbsp (8 g) toasted flour (see page 9)

2 tbsp (30 ml) olive oil

1 onion, finely diced

1 thick (7-oz [200-g]) slice dry cured ham (prosciutto), cut into medium strips (lardons)

3 tbsp (45 ml) tomato paste

¾ cup (200 ml) full-bodied red wine

2 cloves garlic, bruised

1 bay leaf

2 sprigs thyme

9 oz (250 g) canned whole peeled tomatoes

1 cup (150 g) green olives, pitted or unpitted

2 tbsp (30 ml) cognac

MISE EN PLACE

You will need a Dutch oven or cast-iron pot. If using, make the Brown Chicken Stock in advance according to the recipe on page 13. Bring the stock to a light boil and set aside. Season the inside of the chicken with salt and pepper, then tie the ends of the chicken legs together with kitchen twine. Preheat the oven to 350°F (180°C). Toast the flour according to page 9.

In the pot, heat the oil over medium heat and sear the chicken evenly on all sides until light brown, then transfer to a plate. Add the onion and cured ham to the pot and cook, stirring occasionally, for 5 minutes, then sprinkle with the toasted flour.

In a small bowl, stir the tomato paste and wine together, then pour this mixture into the pot, stirring well to combine with the onion and cured ham. Add the garlic, bay leaf and thyme and bring to a light boil for 3 minutes to allow the liquid to reduce.

Place the chicken and any accumulated juices back into the pot and add the tomatoes. Top with the stock, and bring to a boil before removing from the heat. Cover and first cook in the oven for 30 minutes, then turn the chicken over and stir in the olives. Continue to cook for 20 minutes, or until the chicken is cooked through. (When ready, the chicken thigh's internal temperature should be at least 165°F [74°C]).

Remove the chicken and carve it into four or more pieces, then return the chicken to the pot and finish cooking on the stove. Stir in the cognac and adjust the seasoning to your taste. Simmer, uncovered, for a final 5 to 10 minutes before serving.

RED WINE BEEF RAGOUT DAUPHINOISE

From southeast France, Beef Dauphinoise is a style of preparing beef akin to that of the famous bœuf bourguignon, where the beef is slow-cooked in red wine. But this Provençal version takes the flavor up a notch with the addition of pork rind, cognac and tomatoes. A red wine ragout is always better the next day, so this is a dish you can prepare a day in advance.

Serves 4–6

3½ lb (1½ kg) beef suited for slow-cooking (chuck or blade), cut into large cubes

Salt and pepper, to season

7 oz (200 g) pork rind, in 1 piece

2 tbsp (15 g) toasted flour (see page 9)

2 tbsp (30 ml) cooking oil

3 tbsp (45 ml) cognac

5.5 oz (150 g) smoked bacon, cut into large strips (lardons)

2 medium onions, sliced

2 cloves garlic, bruised

2 medium carrots, sliced

3 tomatoes, quartered

1 sprig thyme

1 bay leaf

1 (25-fl oz [750-ml]) bottle red wine (medium to full-bodied)

2 tbsp (6 g) chopped fresh parsley, to garnish

MISE EN PLACE

You will need a Dutch oven or cast-iron pot. Season the beef with salt and pepper and blanch the pork rind in boiling water for 5 minutes, then rinse and set aside. Preheat the oven to 300°F (150°C). Toast the flour according to page 9.

In the pot, heat the oil over high heat, then add the beef, searing on all sides until dark brown. Mix in the cognac, then transfer the meat and precious cooking juices to a large bowl.

To the same pot, add the bacon, onions and garlic, and sizzle for 3 minutes over medium heat. Stir in the carrots, tomatoes, thyme and bay leaf, and cook for 2 minutes, or until fragrant. Return the meat to the pot, add the pork rind and sprinkle with the toasted flour, stirring all the ingredients together.

Empty the bottle of wine into the pot, stirring gently, and top with water if necessary to ensure the meat is just about covered in liquid. Bring to a boil, then scoop off any foam forming at the surface and remove from the heat. Cover and cook in the oven for 2½ to 3 hours, or until the meat is tender and falls apart easily when prodded with a fork. Discard the bay leaf and thyme and spoon everything else into a serving dish. Garnish with the parsley and serve with a side of rice, potatoes or tagliatelle.

POULET SAUTÉ ALICE

My favorite recipes are those that require minimum effort but bring maximum taste to the table, and this recipe fits the bill. Inspired by the classic *poulet à la crème et aux champignons* (chicken with cream and mushrooms), this dish is Auguste Escoffier's more elegant version. Instead of making the recipe more complicated to elevate the taste, he just added a few extra ingredients, such as stock, wine and a dash of cognac. This dish is simple to make, but you need good-quality brown chicken stock, white wine and cognac to achieve the rich, layered taste that Escoffier intended.

Serves 4

For the Chicken
2 chicken breasts
2 chicken thighs
Salt and pepper, to season
3 tbsp (45 g) unsalted butter
1 tbsp (15 ml) olive oil

For the Sauce
¾ cup (200 ml) Homestyle Demi-Glace (page 15) or Brown Chicken Stock (page 13)
1 tbsp (15 ml) olive oil
5 button mushrooms, quartered
Salt and pepper, to season
1 shallot, finely diced
⅓ cup (80 ml) dry white wine (sauvignon blanc or pinot gris)
2 tbsp (30 ml) cognac
½ cup (120 ml) heavy cream
1 tbsp (3 g) chopped fresh parsley, to garnish

MISE EN PLACE
You will need a Dutch oven or cast-iron pot. Season the chicken with salt and pepper and preheat the oven to 120°F (50°C). Make the Homestyle Demi-Glace or Brown Chicken Stock in advance according to the recipe on page 15 or page 13.

To make the chicken, in the pot, heat the butter and oil over medium heat. When the butter starts to foam, arrange the chicken pieces in the pan without overlapping. Sear the chicken pieces, without turning them, for 8 to 10 minutes, or until golden brown. Then, flip each piece over and cook for 8 minutes. Transfer the chicken to a plate and pour over any butter left in the pan. Cover and keep warm in the oven while you prepare the mushrooms and the sauce.

To make the sauce, in a small skillet, heat the oil over medium heat and sauté the mushrooms, tossing occasionally, until lightly colored. Season with salt and pepper. Remove from the heat and set aside.

Place the same pot used to cook the chicken over medium-high heat and wait for the brown bits at the bottom to caramelize. Add the shallot and sautéed mushrooms (reserve some mushrooms for garnish) and cook for 1 minute, stirring gently, before pouring in the wine and cognac. Let the sauce reduce for 3 minutes, add the demi-glace or stock, then reduce again for 5 minutes to really concentrate the flavor. Stir in the cream and adjust the seasoning with a pinch or two of pepper.

Lower the heat to medium and return the chicken thighs to the pot to finish cooking in the sauce for 10 minutes. Now add the chicken breasts and cook for 5 minutes.

Before serving, check the consistency of the sauce. If it's on the thin side, remove the chicken from the pot and reduce the sauce over high heat for 2 to 3 minutes. To serve, divide the chicken among plates and drench with the sauce. Garnish with a handful of sautéed mushrooms and the parsley.

CREAMY SAUTÉED CHICKEN
WITH CIDER AND CALVADOS

If you've ever wondered why there's so much cream in French recipes, Normandy is to blame. This is where the best cream comes from in France, and it's got the rest of us completely addicted. Normandy is also the French headquarters of apples, Calvados and hard apple cider. If you haven't tried Calvados before, it's a strong apple brandy enjoyed as a digestif in France but also features heavily in Norman recipes. This dish is a fine example of how the Normans bring these ingredients together for an explosion of flavor.

Serves 4

For the Chicken
2 lb (1 kg) chicken pieces (breast, thighs or legs)
Salt and pepper, to season
1 tbsp (8 g) all-purpose flour
1 tbsp (15 ml) cooking oil
1 tbsp (15 g) unsalted butter
½ cup (120 ml) hard apple cider

For the Garnish
2 apples
¼ cup (60 g) butter, divided
5 button mushrooms, stalks removed, quartered
5.5 oz (150 g) bacon, cut into medium-sized strips (lardons)

For the Sauce
2 tbsp (20 g) finely diced shallot
2 tbsp (30 ml) Calvados
½ cup (120 ml) hard apple cider
¾ cup (200 ml) heavy cream or crème fraiche

MISE EN PLACE
Use a Dutch oven or cast-iron pot. Season the chicken with salt and pepper and lightly dust with the flour. Peel, core and halve the apples. Preheat the oven to 350°F (180°C).

To make the chicken, in the pot, heat the oil and butter over medium heat and sear the chicken, turning the pieces over regularly to achieve an even, golden color. Pour the cider over the chicken, then cover and cook for 35 to 40 minutes in the oven. The chicken breasts will cook faster than the rest, so remove them after 15 minutes and set aside covered with foil.

While the chicken cooks, prepare the garnish. In a medium-sized skillet, melt 2 tablespoons (30 g) of the butter over medium heat and sauté the mushrooms until golden, then set aside. Use the same pan to panfry the lardons until golden and add them to the resting mushrooms. Now cut the apples into thin slices and, in a nonstick skillet, sauté them over medium heat in the remaining butter for 5 minutes, or until lightly colored.

By now the chicken should be cooked. Remove the pot from the oven and ladle out the remaining chicken pieces and set them aside with the breasts. When done, transfer all the cooking juice to a small bowl.

To make the sauce, place the same pot over medium-high heat and add the shallot. Cook for 1 minute before adding the Calvados and the cider. Scrape the bottom of the pot gently with a spoon and let the liquid reduce for 3 minutes, or until it becomes somewhat syrupy. Add the reserved chicken-cooking juices and the cream and reduce again for 5 minutes, or until the sauce is thick enough to coat the back of a spoon.

Lower the heat to medium and stir in the bacon and mushrooms along with half of the sautéed apples. Follow by adding the chicken pieces along with any accumulated juices, and adjust the seasoning.

Finally, allow the chicken to warm up in the sauce for 5 minutes before serving on a dish, garnished with a scattering of sautéed apples. For a touch of elegance, serve with Duchess Potatoes (page 170).

DISHES FROM THE SEA

French people are not just particular about the food they eat; they're also particular about where they eat it. When it comes to fish and seafood, coastal towns are usually the only place where one would confidently eat fish. In France, it's not really common to buy and prepare a whole fish hundreds of miles from the sea; however, over time, people from the inland have grown to trust fish filets, scallops and mussels. So, in this chapter, I want to share these recipes based on the fish and shellfish most commonly found at fishmongers, so you can experience the versatility of these flavors wherever you live. There's a range of dishes from the sea: from the classic Marinière Mussels with Pommes Frites (page 145) and Fish and Scallops à la Mornay (page 153) to Bistro Fish Filets with Sautéed Potatoes (page 150) and Poached Fish in Tomato and Vermouth Sauce (page 149). We'll cover breading, panfrying, poaching and crafting the tastiest of sauces using fish cooking juices, wine and cream.

MARINIÈRE MUSSELS WITH POMMES FRITES

Marinière (sailor's) mussels with french fries (or *moules frites*, as we call them) is a much-loved bistro dish enjoyed in towns scattered along the French coast where fresh mussels are abundant. But are French fries actually French? We've all but conceded that these thin, crispy fries did in fact originate from Belgium, which also deserves credit for the genius idea of serving fries and mussels together with a glass of Belgian beer. We're pleased that this dish made its way across the border. It's the perfect down-to-earth dish to enjoy with friends over a glass of good-quality beer and a major sporting event on the television in the background.

Serves 4

2 lb (1 kg) starchy potatoes, scrubbed

4 lb (2 kg) fresh mussels

¼ cup (60 g) unsalted butter

6 tbsp (60 g) finely chopped shallot

¼ cup (12 g) chopped fresh parsley

¼ cup (60 ml) dry white wine

2 pinches of freshly ground pepper

MISE EN PLACE

Prepare a deep fryer with 2 to 3 quarts (2 to 3 L) of cooking oil, depending on the size of the fryer, to cook the fries. You'll also need a large pot (or two medium-sized pots) to cook the mussels. Cut the potatoes into thin fries. (A French fry cutter will do the job much faster.) Then rinse well and let them sit in a bowl of cold water. Wash and scrub the mussels to remove any grit stuck to the shells and cut the hairlike seaweed protruding from the clasp of the mussel. (We call this the beard.)

To precook the fries, bring the temperature of the oil to 320°F (160°C). Drain and pat dry the potatoes, then place them in the fryer basket and plunge them into the hot oil. Cook for 4 minutes, then remove the basket and drain. Now, set the oil temperature to 375°F (190°C) in preparation for the second cooking.

To cook the mussels, in a large pot, melt the butter and combine the shallot, parsley, wine and pepper over high heat. Bring the liquid to a boil and stir in the mussels with a wooden spoon to coat well in the mixture. Cover and let steam on high heat for 5 minutes, shaking the pot around at regular intervals. Turn off the heat and turn your attention back to the fries.

Plunge the fries back into the oil to cook a second time for 3 to 5 minutes, or until crisp and golden, and then allow to drain on a paper towel–lined plate.

To serve, scoop the mussels into four deep plates, ladle a small amount of juice over each portion and stack some fries on the side. Bring everything to the table and enjoy with some beer on the side. Don't forget an extra dish to catch the empty shells.

VARIATION

Normandy-style: Replace the wine with hard apple cider and add 3 tablespoons (45 ml) of cream to the mussel juices to create a quick creamy sauce.

Belgium-style: Replace the shallot with the same quantity of onion and add an equal amount of finely chopped celery.

TIP

Before serving, pass the mussel cooking juices through a fine mesh sieve to discard any hard residue.

BREADED FISH FILETS WITH TARTARE SAUCE

Something as simple as breading fish still takes a little technique to achieve a delicious result. The three-step breading method used in this recipe is exactly how you attain breaded filets that are moist and tender on the inside with a crispy exterior that begs for a sauce to be dipped in. And when it comes to sauces for fish, you can't beat a fragrant tartare made with homemade mayonnaise, chopped fresh herbs and pickles. A simple but delicious formula that never gets old.

Serves 4

For the Tartare Sauce
1 batch Homemade Mayonnaise (page 22)
2 tbsp (20 g) finely chopped gherkins
1½ tbsp (15 g) finely chopped capers in brine
1 tbsp (3 g) finely chopped mixed fresh herbs (parsley, tarragon, chives or chervil)
1 tsp (2 g) finely sliced green onion (spring onion)
1 tsp finely chopped shallot
Pinch of cayenne pepper
Salt and pepper, to season

For the Fish
1 lb (500 g) fish filets, whole or cut in strips
½ cup (60 g) all-purpose flour
2 large eggs, beaten
3.5 oz (100 g) breadcrumbs
Salt and pepper, to season
3 tbsp (45 ml) cooking oil, plus an extra dash to finish cooking the filets

MISE EN PLACE
Make the Homemade Mayonnaise according to the recipe on page 22. Clean, trim and dry the fish filets with a paper towel.

To make the tartare sauce, place the mayonnaise in a small bowl and stir in the gherkins, capers, herbs, green onion, shallot and cayenne. Season to your liking, then cover and tuck the sauce away in the fridge while you prepare the fish.

Time to set up your breading station: Take three plates large enough to accommodate the filets, and line them up. Place the flour in the first, the beaten eggs in the second and then the breadcrumbs in the third. Now, let the breading begin. Season the filets with salt and pepper, and then, working with one piece at a time, coat the fish in the flour, then dip in the eggs before coating in the breadcrumbs.

In a large, stainless-steel or nonstick skillet, heat the oil over medium heat (to prevent burning the breadcrumbs). When the oil flows like water, lay the filets beside each other, leaving some breathing space in between (cook in batches if your pan is too small to fit them all).

Gently cook the filets on one side for 4 minutes, or until golden and crisp, and then flip them over, add an extra dash of oil and cook the second side for 4 to 5 minutes. Transfer to a paper towel–lined plate to drain any excess oil before serving.

To create a relaxed and casual bistro experience, I love serving the fish filets piled in a large dish garnished with a few lemon quarters and the bowl of tartare sauce on the side for everyone to help themselves. Don't forget fresh salad and a large bowl of fries.

TIP
Use this same breading technique for meat, seafood and vegetables.

POACHED FISH IN TOMATO AND VERMOUTH SAUCE

There's more than one way to poach a fish. This recipe uses the common French cooking technique of shallow poaching (*cuisson à court mouillement*), whereby the fish is poached in a shallow liquid that is then used as a base to craft a flavorful sauce. The sauce uses a reduction of onion, tomato, cream, fish stock, white wine and some white vermouth for a touch of class. I use cod, but haddock, halibut or any flaky fish will work, too.

Serves 4

For the Tomato and Onion Reduction

7 oz (200 g) whole peeled canned tomatoes

2 tbsp (30 g) unsalted butter, cut into small cubes

½ cup (80 g) finely diced onion

1 bay leaf

1 sprig thyme

Salt and pepper, to season

For the Fish

¾ cup (200 ml) Quick Seafood Stock (page 16) or good-quality premade fish stock

4 (5.5 oz [150 g]) filets fresh cod or other white fish

Salt and pepper, to season

1 small shallot, finely diced

2 tbsp (30 ml) French sauvignon blanc (dry white wine)

2 tbsp (30 g) butter, cut in small cubes

For the Sauce

½ cup (120 ml) heavy cream

1 tbsp (15 ml) Noilly Prat (French white vermouth)

2 tbsp (6 g) chopped fresh parsley

MISE EN PLACE

Drain the tomatoes through a fine-mesh sieve over a bowl, then remove and discard the seeds and chop the tomatoes finely. If using, make the Quick Seafood Stock in advance according to the recipe on page 16. Bring the stock to a light boil and set aside. Clean, trim and season the fish filets. Preheat the oven to 120°F (50°C).

To make the tomato and onion reduction, in a medium-sized saucepan, melt the butter over low heat and stir in the onion to coat evenly. Sauté the onion for 10 minutes, or until soft and translucent. Add the tomatoes, bay leaf, thyme and a pinch each of salt and pepper, stirring the ingredients gently. Cook for 5 minutes, or until the tomatoes melt into a puree, then set aside.

To cook the fish, scatter the diced shallot into a large sauté pan and lay the filets on top. Pour in the stock and wine and sprinkle the butter cubes on top. Cover the fish with parchment paper and bring to a simmer over medium heat. When the liquid starts to simmer, lower the heat slightly to prevent boiling and continue to cook for 10 to 15 minutes (depending on the thickness of the filets), or until cooked through and tender. Transfer the filets to a plate and spoon some of the cooking juices over to keep them moist. Cover with parchment paper and keep warm in the oven while you make the sauce.

To prepare the sauce, drain the rest of the cooking liquid through a fine-mesh sieve into the pan that contains the tomato reduction, then add the cream and bring to a light boil. Reduce for 10 minutes or more, until the sauce thickens to coat the back of a spoon. Taste and correct the seasoning, add the accumulated fish juices from the resting fish and stir in the Noilly Prat.

To serve, slide the filets onto a warm serving dish, smother in the sauce and garnish with the parsley. Enjoy with French-Style Pilaf Rice (page 161) or a tagliatelle pasta to soak up the umami sauce.

BISTRO FISH FILETS WITH SAUTÉED POTATOES

If you've ever wondered how the French approach English fish and chips, this dish would be it. In typical French flair, the fish is panfried or grilled, instead of deep-fried, and served on a bed of lightly sautéed potatoes with onions, shallots, parsley and a splash of vinegar. This dish is certainly a healthier substitute for Friday night fish and chips . . . and tastier too. I recommend using a fish with firm flesh, such as snapper, cod or swordfish.

Serves 4

For the Fish
4 (5.5 oz [150 g]) firm-fleshed fish filets

Salt and pepper, to season

1 tbsp (15 ml) olive oil

3 tbsp (45 ml) white wine vinegar

2 tbsp (6 g) chopped fresh parsley, to garnish

For the Sautéed Potatoes
6 medium-sized yellow waxy potatoes, scrubbed and unpeeled

2 tbsp (30 g) coarse salt

2 tbsp (30 g) unsalted butter

2 onions, finely sliced

2 shallots, finely sliced

1 tbsp (15 ml) olive oil

Salt and pepper, to season

MISE EN PLACE
Clean and trim the fish filets and set aside on a plate.

To make the potatoes, place the potatoes (skin on) into a large saucepan and fill with cold water. Add the salt and bring to a boil over high heat. Once the water starts to boil, lower the heat to medium and set a timer for 20 minutes.

While the potatoes are cooking, in a large nonstick skillet, melt the butter over medium-low heat. Sauté the onions and shallots, stirring gently, for 10 minutes, or until they're glossy and lightly colored, and then set aside.

When the potatoes are cooked, drain and let them cool before peeling and cutting them into roughly ¾-inch (2-cm)–thick slices. In the same skillet, heat the oil over medium heat and sauté the potatoes with a pinch each of salt and pepper for 10 minutes, tossing occasionally. (It's not the intention here to brown or sear the potatoes; aim for a light golden color.) When done, turn off the heat and let the potatoes rest in the skillet while you cook the fish.

To cook the fish, simply season the filets with salt and pepper and brush each side with the oil, then grill or panfry according to your preference. (A nonstick pan is recommended for panfrying.) The total cooking time should be about 10 minutes.

While the fish is cooking, place the pan of sautéed potatoes over medium heat and sprinkle with the onion and shallot mixture. Toss well and cook for 5 minutes. Serve the fish on plates with a side of potatoes. For the bistro touch, pour the vinegar into the same skillet used to cook the potatoes and swirl to collect the leftover cooking juices. Then, pour it over the fish, sprinkle with parsley and your French-style fish and chips are ready. Bon appétit.

FISH AND SCALLOPS À LA MORNAY

These seashells à la Mornay will add a touch of elegance to any dinner party without too much effort. Scallop shells are filled with fish flakes poached in white wine and seared scallops, and then dressed in a béchamel-based sauce and Gruyère cheese before being placed under the broiler for crispy, melted goodness. This charming starter will go down well with a glass of white wine, such as a Chablis. You can replace the scallops with clams, shrimp or even lobster, if feeling particularly fancy.

Serves 4

For the Fish

½ cup (120 ml) Quick Seafood Stock (page 16) or good-quality premade fish stock

7 oz (200 g) cod or other delicate, flaky fish, trimmed and cleaned

Salt and pepper, to season

2 shallots, finely diced

1 tbsp (3 g) chopped fresh parsley

1 tbsp (15 g) unsalted butter, cut into small cubes

2 tbsp (30 ml) white wine

For the Scallops

4 scallops, rinsed and patted dry

1 tbsp (15 ml) olive oil, plus more for serving

2 tbsp (30 g) unsalted butter

For the Sauce

½ batch of Classic Béchamel (page 23)

3 tbsp (45 ml) cream

Salt and pepper, to season

2 oz (60 g) grated Gruyère or Cheddar cheese

2 tbsp (15 g) breadcrumbs

MISE EN PLACE

For this recipe, you will need four scallop shells, washed and dried, or small baking dishes. If using, make the Quick Seafood Stock in advance according to the recipe on page 16. Bring the stock to a light boil and set aside. Make half a batch of béchamel sauce by halving the ingredients in the recipe on page 23.

To cook the fish, lay the fish down in a medium-sized sauté pan and season with salt and pepper. Sprinkle with the shallots and parsley, then add the butter cubes along with the stock and wine. Cover the fish with parchment paper and bring to a simmer over medium heat.

When the liquid starts to simmer, lower the heat slightly and poach the fish for 8 to 10 minutes, and then transfer to a plate. Coat with 2 tablespoons (30 ml) of cooking juices and let stand, covered. Strain the rest of the cooking juices through a fine-mesh sieve into a bowl and set aside.

To cook the scallops, in a small nonstick pan, sear the scallops in the olive oil over medium heat for 3 minutes, or until golden. Then, turn them over, add the butter and baste the scallops for 2 minutes. Remove from the heat and set aside.

To make the sauce, in a small saucepan, combine the béchamel sauce, cream and the reserved fish cooking juices. Bring to a gentle boil over medium heat, and then reduce for 5 to 8 minutes to thicken and concentrate the flavor. When done, taste and correct the seasoning.

Preheat the oven to broil on a high temperature. To dress the shells or dishes, add a few tablespoons (45 ml) of the sauce, followed by a sprinkle of flaked fish and a scallop. Top with more sauce, grated cheese, 2 pinches of breadcrumbs and a trickle of olive oil. Slide the shells onto a baking sheet and broil for 5 minutes, or until the cheese has melted and the breadcrumbs are golden. Serve immediately.

FISH WITH SAFFRON VELOUTÉ SAUCE

There's nothing out there quite like saffron. Saffron balances that fine line between sweet and savory with an earthy, honeylike flavor and is the key ingredient that gives the famous bouillabaisse that striking golden hue. This recipe uses just a few strands of saffron to elevate a humble fish in a white wine pan sauce into a sumptuous meal.

Serves 4

For the Fish

¾ cup (200 ml) Quick Seafood Stock (page 16) or a good-quality premade fish stock

4 (5.5 oz [150 g]) pieces white fish, such as halibut, cod or seabass

Salt and pepper, to season

2 tbsp (20 g) finely diced shallot

2 tbsp (30 ml) French sauvignon blanc (or dry white wine)

1 bay leaf

1 sprig thyme

2 tbsp (30 g) unsalted butter, cut into small cubes

For the Sauce

2 tbsp (30 g) unsalted butter

1 clove garlic, finely diced

3 tbsp (30 g) finely diced shallot

1 tbsp (8 g) all-purpose flour

1 tbsp (15 ml) good-quality tomato coulis (page 29) or passata

2 pinches of finely cut saffron threads

½ cup (120 ml) heavy cream

MISE EN PLACE

If using, make the Quick Seafood Stock in advance according to the recipe on page 16. Bring the stock to a light boil and set aside. Trim, clean and season the fish pieces with salt and pepper. Preheat the oven to 120°F (50°C).

To cook the fish, spread the diced shallot around a large stainless-steel sauté pan and lay the filets on top. Pour in the stock and wine, add the bay leaf and thyme and sprinkle the butter cubes over. Cover the fish with parchment paper and bring to a simmer over medium heat. When the liquid starts to simmer, lower the heat slightly to prevent boiling and continue to cook for 10 to 15 minutes, or until the filets are cooked through and tender.

Transfer the fish to a plate and spoon 2 tablespoons (30 ml) of the cooking juices on top. Cover with parchment paper and keep warm in the oven. Strain the remaining cooking juices through a fine-mesh sieve into a bowl and reserve for the sauce.

To make the sauce, in a medium-sized saucepan over low heat, combine the butter, garlic and shallot and cook for 3 minutes, stirring occasionally, before adding the flour and cooking for a further 2 minutes. Now, stir in the tomato coulis, saffron and the reserved fish cooking juices. Cook gently for 3 minutes, or until the sauce thickens. Then stir in the cream, increase the heat to medium and wait for the sauce to come back to a simmer. Reduce for at least 5 minutes, or until the sauce thickens to coat the back of a spoon. Return the fish and accumulated juices back to the sauté pan used to cook the fish and strain the sauce over. Gently baste for 2 minutes, or until the fish is warm enough to serve.

OVEN-BAKED FISH WITH
WHITE VERMOUTH *À LA MINUTE*

In home cooking, *à la minute* refers to a recipe that can be made in a flash, and this recipe is a fine example. This fish *à la minute* is a gratifying way to cook fresh fish filets in a one-pot fashion without sacrificing taste. Use any fish with a flaky texture (e.g., cod, halibut or rockling) and bake in the winning combination of shallot, white vermouth, white wine, parsley and olive oil with a sprinkle of breadcrumbs. It's the answer to those long days where you need something fast, light and tasty.

Serves 4

4 (5.5-oz [150-g])-thick fish filets, or 1 large (21-oz [600-g]) filet cut into 4 pieces

1 tbsp (15 ml) olive oil

2 tbsp (20 g) finely diced shallot

1 tbsp (3 g) chopped fresh curly parsley

Salt and pepper, to season

2 tbsp (30 ml) Noilly Prat (white vermouth)

½ cup (120 ml) dry white wine

3 tbsp (20 g) breadcrumbs

2 tbsp (30 g) unsalted butter, cut into small cubes

3 tbsp (45 ml) heavy cream (optional)

MISE EN PLACE

Clean and trim the fish filets and use a sharp knife to make light crisscross incisions on the skin side. Preheat the oven to 425°F (220°C).

Coat a large baking dish with the olive oil and lay in the fish filets, skin side down. Scatter with the shallot and parsley and season generously with salt and pepper. Pour the vermouth and wine over the fish and sprinkle the top of each filet with a layer of breadcrumbs followed by the butter cubes. Place in the oven and bake for 20 to 25 minutes, depending on the thickness of the fish. When done, the fish should be cooked through and the breadcrumbs beautifully crisp and golden. Optionally, for a creamy sauce, stir in the cream with the cooking juices before serving. Enjoy fresh out of the oven with any kind of side.

CLASSIC AND REGIONAL SIDES

It's easy to rest on your laurels when it comes to pairing side dishes with a main. Often, so much thought and attention has gone into preparing the culinary centerpiece that we fall back on the same tried-and-true sidekicks. This chapter is designed to bring more variety to your table without complicating things, and features simple, delicious sides, such as French-Style Pilaf Rice (page 161) and Potato Gratin with Mushrooms (page 169), which are easy to scale up for seasonal feasts. These dishes will pair well with most of the mains in this book, so there's no need to scratch your head trying to work out the perfect combination. You may want to rotate recipes to discover your favorite combinations or work your way through to discover how each side brings something special to the table. There are no rules, really; just choose sides when the main vegetable is in season, and you can't fail.

FRENCH-STYLE PILAF RICE

Cooking rice seems so simple, but it is hard to get it right every time, and usually results in overcooked, undercooked or just plain mushy rice. To escape these rice-cooking woes, here's the easy method to ensure perfectly cooked rice every time. This recipe is foolproof, and with just a hint of savory fragrance, it complements most French mains without competing for flavor.

Serves 4

1¼ cups (300 ml) water, White Chicken Stock (page 12) or good quality premade stock

3 tbsp (45 g) butter, plus an extra dab to finish the rice

½ cup (80 g) finely diced onion

7 oz (200 g) long-grain rice (jasmine)

1 bay leaf

1 sprig thyme

Salt and pepper, to season

MISE EN PLACE

I recommend using a large ovenproof sauté pan or pot with a lid for this recipe. If using, make the White Chicken Stock in advance according to the recipe on page 12. Bring the stock to a light boil and set aside. Prepare a paper lid (*cartouche*) by cutting a circle of parchment paper to the diameter of your pan. Preheat the oven to 375°F (190°C).

Place a large sauté pan over low heat and melt the butter, then stir in the onion and cook gently for 2 minutes, or until fragrant. Add the rice, mixing well so that the grains are well coated, and continue to cook for 2 minutes. Pour the warm water or stock gently over the rice, add the bay leaf and thyme and season with salt and pepper. Increase the heat to high to quickly bring the liquid to a simmer, then immediately switch the heat off.

Place the cartouche inside the pan so that it rests on the rice. Cover with a lid and slide the pan onto the middle rack of the oven. Set a timer to cook for 17 minutes. When the time is up, taste the rice to check whether it's done; it should be tender and well puffed. If not, return it to the oven for a few more minutes. When cooked, let the rice stand, covered, for 5 minutes.

Just before serving the rice, discard the cartouche, bay leaf and thyme, and to finish, stir through a dab of butter. Use a fork to separate and loosen the grains a little before enjoying with your favorite main dish.

VARIATION

This pilaf is versatile; you can add all sorts of extra ingredients to enhance the flavor. For example, when you start cooking the onion, add any of the following: sautéed meat, diced vegetables, mushrooms, spices or herbs. For a golden rice, add ½ teaspoon of ground turmeric when pouring in the water or stock.

LYONNAISE SAUTÉED GREEN BEANS

This regional method of cooking green beans is popular in the town of Lyon in southeast France. Commonly paired with steaks, this recipe demonstrates just how simple and flavorful French side dishes can be. The green beans are first boiled, then sautéed in onion and butter and then finished with a splash of vinegar. It's a refreshing way to serve green beans with just a hint of tartness to help cut through a heartier main dish.

Serves 4

14 oz (400 g) fresh green beans, ends trimmed

2 tbsp (30 g) coarse salt

2 tbsp (30 g) unsalted butter

1 onion, finely diced

Salt and pepper, to season

1 tbsp (3 g) chopped fresh parsley

2 tbsp (30 ml) good-quality white or red wine vinegar

Bring a large pot of water to boil. Plunge the beans into the pot of boiling water with the coarse salt. Cook, uncovered, for 6 to 8 minutes. When cooked, plunge the beans into a bowl of cold water, then drain through a sieve over a bowl.

In a large skillet, melt the butter over medium heat, add the onion and cook for 5 minutes, or until fragrant and lightly colored. Mix the beans in with the onion, season with salt and pepper to taste and sauté for 5 minutes, or until the onion is golden. Sprinkle in the parsley, then transfer the beans to a serving plate.

Using the same pan, increase the heat to high and wait 2 minutes for the pan to become very hot before adding the vinegar. To deglaze, swish the vinegar around the pan to collect any leftover bits of onion, then pour over the green beans before serving.

CLASSIC CAULIFLOWER GRATIN

This creamy, cheesy cauliflower gratin makes for a decadent side to a light meat or fish main. Cauliflower florets are baked in a luscious *sauce crème* (béchamel sauce with a touch of cream) and smothered in crispy Gruyère cheese. What's not to love? Take care to ensure there are enough crispy bits of cheese to go around so that no guest is left wanting. If you're seeking an alternative to béchamel sauce, try the savory almond custard version in the recipe variation.

Serves 4–6

1 batch Classic Béchamel (page 23)

1 medium-sized cauliflower

2 tbsp (30 g) coarse salt

½ cup (120 ml) heavy cream

2 oz (60 g) grated Gruyère or Cheddar cheese, plus extra to sprinkle over the top of the gratin

Salt and pepper, to season

2 tbsp (30 g) butter, cut into small cubes

MISE EN PLACE

Make the béchamel sauce according to the recipe on page 23 and let it rest in the saucepan. Cut the stalk off the cauliflower and separate into bite-sized florets, then rinse under running water. Preheat the oven to 400°F (200°C). Grease a baking dish with butter.

Bring a large pot of water to a boil. Add the cauliflower florets with the coarse salt and cook, uncovered, for 8 minutes. Then, carefully pour the florets into a colander to drain and set aside.

To make the *sauce crème*, take the saucepan of prepared béchamel sauce and stir in the cream. Bring to a simmer over medium heat, stirring constantly, then cook for 5 minutes over low heat, stirring occasionally. Add the grated cheese and stir until it has melted into the sauce, then remove from the heat.

To make the gratin, arrange the florets in a single layer in the greased baking dish. Sprinkle with salt and pepper, then spoon the sauce evenly over the top. Finish with a sprinkle of grated cheese and the butter cubes. Place the baking dish on the middle rack of the oven and bake for 25 minutes, or until the sauce is bubbling away and the cheese is golden and crisp.

VARIATION

If you don't have time to make béchamel sauce, replace with a savory almond custard: In a bowl, whisk two large eggs with 1 cup (250 ml) of heavy cream, 3 tablespoons (20 g) of almond meal, 2 pinches of freshly grated nutmeg and a pinch each of salt and pepper. Pour over the cauliflower before adding the cheese and bake for 25 minutes at 400°F (200°C).

SAUTÉED POTATOES IN DUCK FAT

Cooking potatoes in duck fat is a long-held tradition in every part of France where duck and geese are farmed, especially around the medieval town of Sarlat in the Dordogne region. This recipe is very simple, with only four ingredients: potatoes, duck fat, garlic and parsley. This combination produces one of the most satisfying, comforting potato dishes on the planet, with the duck fat doing something magical to give the potatoes a delicious richness. It's a glorious side to include on a festive table during the colder months. Pick your potatoes well; only top-quality, yellow-fleshed potatoes will do.

Serves 4

½ cup (120 ml) duck or goose fat, divided

2 lb (1 kg) yellow waxy potatoes, scrubbed

Salt and pepper, to season

3 cloves garlic, finely diced

3 tbsp (9 g) finely chopped fresh parsley

MISE EN PLACE

The quality of the duck or goose fat makes a real difference to this recipe. If possible, try to source it from a specialty food store. Cut the potatoes into medium-sized slices using a mandolin or food processor, rinse in cold water and pat dry.

Pour ¼ cup (60 ml) of the fat into a large stainless-steel or cast-iron skillet over high heat. When the fat is hot, add the potatoes and season well with salt and pepper. Sear for 10 minutes, stirring regularly, then lower the heat to medium. Add the rest of the fat and continue to shallow-fry for 10 minutes, or until the potatoes are tender to the bite and golden.

Remove the excess fat, then adjust the heat to low and sprinkle the garlic and parsley over the potatoes, tossing the pan energetically to mix the ingredients. Cook for 2 minutes to diffuse the flavors before serving.

TIP

You can store duck fat in the freezer for up to a year. Save it for special occasions in the colder months.

POTATO GRATIN WITH MUSHROOMS

This take on the timeless potato gratin is enjoyed in French homes during the autumn months. When perfectly cooked potatoes soften to absorb the cream and mushroom juices, the result is delightful. You can have fun varying the type of mushrooms, but porcini mushrooms (*cèpes*) or morels are first on my list, as they bring an earthy character to the dish, but even good old button mushrooms work wonderfully. You can also do away with mushrooms altogether and use this recipe to make a foolproof classic potato gratin.

Serves 4–6

For the Mushroom Garnish
2 tbsp (30 g) unsalted butter

7 oz (200 g) mushrooms (your favorite variety), chopped or sliced

Salt and pepper, to season

1 clove garlic, finely chopped

2 tbsp (6 g) chopped fresh parsley

For the Gratin
1 clove garlic, finely chopped

Salt and pepper, to season

2 lb (1 kg) all-purpose potatoes, scrubbed

Few pinches of freshly grated nutmeg

1²/₃ cups (400 ml) heavy cream

MISE EN PLACE
I recommend using a medium-sized baking dish with high sides (I used an oval dish around 7 x 11 inches [18 x 28 cm]). Hold off peeling and cutting the potatoes for now; we'll do this just before we layer them in the dish. Grease a baking dish with butter.

To make the mushroom garnish, in a large skillet, melt the butter over medium heat, then add the mushrooms and season with salt and pepper. Toss well to coat evenly in the butter and sauté for 5 minutes, or until the mushrooms are golden brown. Add the garlic and parsley and toss together. Cook for 1 minute, and then set aside.

To prepare the gratin, sprinkle the garlic over the bottom of the greased baking dish along with a few pinches each of salt and pepper. Peel and cut the potatoes into thin slices and divide them into two equal portions. Arrange the first portion of potatoes in the baking dish in layers, seasoning each layer generously with salt, pepper and a pinch of nutmeg. Then, spread the mushroom garnish evenly over the first portion of potatoes. Layer the rest of the potatoes, repeating the same process as above. To finish, slowly pour the cream all over and season once more.

Place the baking dish on the middle rack of the oven. (The oven should *not* be preheated.) Set the temperature to 340°F (170°C). Bake the gratin for 1 hour and 15 minutes, or until the potatoes are golden and feel soft when pricked with a knife. Once cooked, allow to cool until lukewarm (see Note).

NOTE
A potato gratin should only be served lukewarm. Be patient and let it cool for at least 30 minutes to allow the juices to settle and flavors to mingle. This also makes it much easier to slice and serve.

DUCHESS POTATOES

Transform typical mashed potatoes into elegant and delicious crispy potato swirls. Duchess potatoes are an easy and sophisticated way to upgrade any main dish. Using a piping bag, you can create beautiful shapes, such as crispy swirls and fluffy rosettes, with a simple mixture of mashed potatoes and egg yolks.

Makes 10–15, depending on size

2 lb (1 kg) starchy potatoes suited for mashing, scrubbed

2 tbsp (30 g) coarse salt

½ cup (120 g) unsalted butter, plus 2 tbsp (30 ml) melted (optional)

Salt and pepper, to season

Pinch of freshly grated nutmeg

4 large egg yolks, beaten

MISE EN PLACE

You will need a food mill or potato ricer, and a piping bag fitted with a large star tip. Line a baking sheet with parchment paper. Preheat the oven to 350°F (180°C).

Place the potatoes in a large saucepan of cold water. Add the coarse salt and bring to a boil, then lower the heat to medium and cook the potatoes for 15 to 20 minutes, or until tender but still firm. Drain and allow the potatoes to dry for 5 minutes in a colander before peeling them.

Use the mill to puree the potatoes into a medium-sized saucepan, then dry over low heat and stir in the butter. When fully combined, season to taste with salt and pepper and add the nutmeg. Turn off the heat and use a spoon to gently mix in the beaten egg yolks.

Pack the potato mixture into the piping bag and use some artistic flair to pipe walnut-sized florets, rosettes or any shape you like onto the baking sheet. For a golden touch, you can drizzle a few drops of melted butter over each mound. Bake for 15 to 20 minutes, or until the potatoes are light brown and crisp. Serve immediately to beautify almost any main dish.

VARIATION

Enhance the flavor by adding herbs, spices or cheese to the potato puree.

TIP

Use the same mixture to make potato croquettes by piping 2-inch (5-cm)-long log shapes with a straight piping tip or by rolling the mixture into walnut-sized balls. Use the breading technique on page 146 to coat the potatoes with all-purpose flour, beaten egg and breadcrumbs. Deep fry the croquettes for 5 minutes in oil at 350°F (180°C), then drain on a paper towel.

POTATOES BOULANGÈRE

Who said that the French must have cream in everything? These *boulangère* potatoes are just like a classic gratin, but without the cream. The potatoes are slow cooked in an aromatic blend of onions, cooking stock and farmhouse smoked bacon. The result is a hearty dish of tender, melt-in-your mouth potatoes infused with a smoky onion and bacon flavor. This delectable side pairs well with any meat dish.

Serves 4–6

1¼ cups (300 ml) White Chicken Stock (page 12) or good-quality premade chicken stock

2 lb (1 kg) all-purpose potatoes, scrubbed

3 tbsp (40 g) unsalted butter

2 onions, finely sliced

Salt and pepper, to season

7 oz (200 g) smoked bacon, cut into medium-sized cubes or strips (lardons)

1 tbsp (15 ml) olive oil

Few pinches of freshly grated nutmeg

2 cloves garlic, finely diced

1 bay leaf

2 sprigs thyme

MISE EN PLACE

If using, make the White Chicken Stock in advance according to the recipe on page 12. Bring the stock to a light boil and set aside. Cut the potatoes in small quarters or medium-sized cubes, and immerse in a bowl of water. Grease a large baking dish with butter.

In a large skillet, melt the butter over medium-low heat, and sauté the onions with some salt and pepper, stirring regularly until lightly colored, about 10 minutes. Transfer the onions to a bowl.

Use the same skillet to panfry the bacon for 3 minutes (no extra fat needed) until crisp and light brown, then drain on some paper towels. Drain and pat dry the potatoes and place them into a large bowl. Drizzle with the olive oil, season with salt and pepper and add a few pinches of nutmeg. Mix in the bacon and onions to distribute evenly through the potatoes.

Add the garlic, bay leaf and thyme to the baking dish. Fill the dish with the potato mixture and pour the warm stock over. Place the dish in the oven (the oven should *not* be preheated) and set the temperature to 375°F (190°C). Cook, loosely covered with parchment paper, for 1 hour, then remove the parchment paper and cook for 15 minutes, or until most of the liquid is absorbed and the potatoes are crisp on top. Let it stand for 20 minutes before serving.

BRITTANY WHITE BEANS

Dried white, black or red beans look so decorative lined on a shelf in jars, but is it just me, or does no one seem very motivated to cook with them? This recipe will remove that dried beans block by showing just how easy they are to cook and how deliciously rustic they can be. Here, white beans are cooked in a rich Brittany-style tomato sauce made with onion, garlic, herbs and white wine. These beans are appetizing enough to enjoy on their own or as an accompaniment to white meats (e.g., panfried pork, veal or chicken). It's worth reaching to the top of the shelf for those dried beans.

Serves 4

For the Beans

10.5 oz (300 g) dried white beans

4 whole cloves

1 onion, halved

3.5 oz (100 g) pork rind (optional)

1 clove garlic, halved

1 bay leaf

1 sprig thyme

1 carrot, sliced

1 tbsp (15 g) coarse salt

For the Sauce

2 oz (60 g) duck fat, divided

1 onion, chopped

5.5 oz (150 g) smoked bacon, rind removed, cut into thin strips (lardons)

1¼ cups (300 ml) white wine

14 oz (400 g) canned diced tomatoes or passata

1 tbsp (15 ml) tomato paste

1 clove garlic, halved

1 bay leaf

1 sprig thyme

1 tsp sugar

Salt and pepper, to season

1 tbsp (3 g) chopped fresh parsley

MISE EN PLACE

Soak the beans in a bowl of water overnight. Stick 2 cloves into each onion half.

To cook the beans, drain and place them in a large saucepan filled with cold water. Bring to a boil, then adjust the heat to low and remove any foam floating on the surface. Add the clove-studded onion halves, pork rind (if using), garlic, bay leaf, thyme and carrot and cook, uncovered, for 40 minutes. After 30 minutes, add the coarse salt.

To make the sauce, spoon 1 ounce (30 g) of the duck fat into a large saucepan over medium heat, then add the onion and bacon. Cook for 5 minutes, until fragrant, then pour in the white wine and mix well. Increase the heat to high and cook for 10 minutes, or until the liquid reduces by half. Add the diced tomatoes, tomato paste, garlic, bay leaf, thyme, sugar and some salt and pepper to taste. Simmer for 15 minutes, then set aside. When the beans are cooked, drain and discard the aromatics, then add the beans to the tomato sauce along with the remaining duck fat. Mix well, then simmer for 10 minutes before serving with a sprinkle of parsley.

BASQUE-STYLE SAUTÉED COURGETTES

I never cared much for *courgettes* (zucchini) until I spent some time in the Basque country in southwest France. A friend shared a flat with a local chef who introduced me to sautéed courgettes in garlic and parsley. My relationship with this green vegetable changed from this point, and I became a convert. The secret to this dish is to parcook the courgettes by searing them with a touch of olive oil, and then letting them stand on the stove with the heat off to finish cooking in the residual heat. This technique produces firm, seared courgette slices that wear the sautéed garlic and parsley with style. It's simple and it works.

Serves 4

3 medium-sized courgettes (zucchini)
2 tbsp (30 ml) olive oil
Salt and pepper, to season
3 cloves garlic, finely diced
3 tbsp (9 g) finely chopped fresh parsley

MISE EN PLACE

Use a large nonstick skillet so you have ample space to toss the courgettes around when searing them. Cut the courgettes in half lengthwise and slice diagonally into medium slices.

In the skillet, heat the olive oil over high heat, and then add the courgettes. Season well with salt and pepper and sauté, tossing the courgette slices around the pan, for 6 minutes, or until evenly seared. Sprinkle with the garlic and parsley and continue to toss the ingredients for 1 minute before turning off the heat. Now, pop a lid on the pan and let the courgettes stand undisturbed on the stove for 5 minutes to finish cooking in the residual heat before serving.

FRENCH GARDEN PEAS WITH A TWIST

You might be surprised to hear that the French use frozen peas in home cooking without a second thought. Even from a bag, they still have that fresh minty flavor without the labor of shelling hundreds of peas. This classic French recipe never gets old. Peas are cooked in a delicious quartet of butter, onions, lettuce (yes, you read that right) and bacon. Leave out the bacon and add boiled carrots or turnips for a vegetarian option.

Serves 4

1–2 handfuls of butter lettuce

1 tbsp (15 g) coarse salt

1¾ lb (800 g) frozen peas

2 tbsp (30 g) unsalted butter, plus extra to finish (optional)

3.5 oz (100 g) sliced shallot

3.5 oz (100 g) smoked bacon, cut into thin strips or cubes

1 tsp sugar

Salt and pepper, to season

MISE EN PLACE

Wash the lettuce and roll the leaves into cigar shapes before slicing them finely. (This is called a chiffonade.)

Bring a large pot of water to a boil, and add the salt and peas. Cook the peas just until the water returns to a boil, then immediately drain and rinse under cold water. Set aside while you prepare the garnish.

In a medium-sized saucepan, melt the butter over medium heat. Add the shallot and bacon and cook, stirring regularly, for 3 minutes. Mix in the lettuce, sugar and peas and season well with salt and pepper. Cover and simmer for 5 minutes, or until the peas are glossy, giving them a little stir from time to time. For extra indulgence, stir in a dab of butter just before serving.

Part 4: Treats, Tarts and Desserts to Please Everyone

This is the part where you get to make those glorious, sweet things you dream about eating in France. France is renowned for its wonderful desserts and sweets, and it's my strong belief that the belly always holds a special space for dessert, even after a satisfying meal. Possessed of a self-confessed sweet tooth, narrowing the selection of sweets and desserts for this book was no easy feat. There are just so many favorites. But I love to bake by the maxim "minimum effort, maximum pleasure," so we've kept it easy and simple, except for a couple of showstoppers for special occasions. Variety is the objective with such classics as Family-Size Crème Caramel (page 191), Commercy-Style Madeleines (page 188) and Classic Flambéed Crêpes (page 192), along with some unique regional specialties that you've likely never tried before. Many of these sweet delights are perfect for a Sunday baking session and easy enough for the kids to help too.

BAKED COCONUT TREATS

Coconut is one of my favorite ingredients in a dessert. Just the scent conjures thoughts of a faraway tropical island. These gooey, sweet coconut mounds are a regular indulgence of mine, ready to eat in 15 minutes. The amounts listed in the recipe can easily be doubled, or even tripled, because once you start eating these, it's hard to stop. Time to pull out that bag of shredded coconut sitting in the cupboard and put it to good use.

Serves 4

2.1 oz (60 g) egg whites (from 2 large eggs)
5.3 oz (150 g) sugar
5.3 oz (150 g) fine desiccated coconut
½ tsp organic vanilla extract

MISE EN PLACE
Have a food thermometer ready. Preheat the oven to 400°F (200°C) using conventional heat (non-fan force). Line a baking sheet with parchment paper.

Sit a large glass bowl over a small saucepan containing 1 cup (250 ml) of water and bring to a simmer. (Make sure the bowl doesn't touch the water.) In the bowl, combine the egg whites and sugar and whisk gently but constantly until the temperature of the mixture reaches 115°F (45°C). (Use a food thermometer to monitor the temperature.) Move the bowl to a countertop and stir in the coconut and the vanilla extract. Use a wooden spoon to work the ingredients until you get a paste-like consistency.

Dip your fingers in water and use your hands to shape large walnut-sized mounds onto the baking sheet, leaving 1¼ inches (3 cm) between them.

Bake the coconut treats on the middle rack of the oven for 15 to 20 minutes, or until the tops are golden. When ready, remove from the oven and let them rest for 5 minutes before biting into these succulent-tasting goodies.

TIP
For a more rustic look, use a mix of desiccated and shredded coconut.

OLD-FASHIONED MACARONS

Say the word *macarons* and the image that springs to mind is pyramids of colorful biscuits decorating the shop fronts of high-end pâtisseries. While they look stunning, this type of macaron is not so easy to make at home, so here's a much simpler alternative. Back in early 19th-century Paris, the simpler old-style French macaron was all the rage, but it was more of a biscuit than the gooey meringue we know today. You won't believe it only takes a few ingredients and 15 minutes to prepare a batch of these addictive biscuits.

Makes 20–25 macarons, depending on size

3.5 oz (100 g) almond meal
7 oz (200 g) superfine sugar
2.1 oz (60 g) egg whites (from 2 large eggs)
Few drops of bitter almond extract

MISE EN PLACE
You can use a spoon to mound the macarons on the pan, but a piping bag with a large straight tip does the job more neatly. Preheat the oven to 350°F (180°C). Line a baking sheet with parchment paper.

In a bowl, blend together the almond meal and sugar with a wooden spoon. Add the egg whites and mix until the whites are fully absorbed and the mixture becomes a paste.

Now, get ready for a little workout. Spend 3 minutes working the paste vigorously with the wooden spoon, constantly mixing, then flattening the paste against the sides of the bowl to blend the sugar into the paste. Mix in a few drops of almond extract to finish.

Spoon the paste into a piping bag and pipe mounds equal to 1 teaspoon onto the baking sheet, leaving a 1¼ inches (3 cm) of space between the mounds. Use a pastry brush dipped in water to gently moisten the top of each mound.

Bake the macarons for 12 to 15 minutes, or until light brown. Remove from the oven and let them rest for 10 minutes before gently detaching each macaron from the parchment paper. They will keep for several days in an airtight container.

VARIATION
Create modern-style macarons with a filling of chocolate ganache, buttercream or jam.

VANILLA RICE PUDDING WITH RAISINS AND GRAND MARNIER

Let me begin by saying that my rice pudding addiction runs deep, and I have several versions of this classic recipe on rotation. At the time of writing, this iteration with raisins soaked in Grand Marnier is my favorite. To achieve the tastiest and creamiest rice pudding, it's all in the little details. I use Arborio rice and fresh vanilla bean, and stir the egg yolks through the rice toward the end to create a beautiful golden custard. This is best eaten cold and without moderation.

Serves 4–6

1.7 oz (50 g) raisins

3 tbsp (45 ml) Grand Marnier

30.5 fl oz (900 ml) whole milk

4.2 oz (120 g) sugar

Pinch of salt

1 fresh vanilla bean, split in half lengthwise with the seeds scraped

7 oz (200 g) uncooked Arborio rice

2 tbsp (30 g) unsalted butter

2 large egg yolks

3 tbsp (45 ml) heavy cream (optional)

MISE EN PLACE

Soak the raisins in the Grand Marnier for 30 minutes before starting.

In a large saucepan, stir together the milk, sugar and salt. Add the vanilla bean with the seeds and bring to a simmer over medium heat. Meanwhile, bring a medium-sized saucepan of water to a boil and blanch the rice in the boiling water for 2 minutes. When blanched, drain and add the rice to the saucepan of milk, then adjust the heat to low.

Scoop the raisins out of the Grand Marnier and stir them into the rice, reserving the Grand Marnier to use later. Cook the rice, uncovered, stirring occasionally, for 40 to 45 minutes, or until cooked through and tender.

Use a wooden spoon to blend the butter gently through the rice, then immediately remove the saucepan from the heat. Stir in the egg yolks and watch the magic happen as the pudding transforms into a pale-yellow custard. Drizzle over the reserved Grand Marnier and give the rice a final stir. Discard the vanilla pods and pour the rice pudding into a large baking dish to allow it to cool quickly. When lukewarm, cover with a piece of plastic wrap that sits in direct contact with the surface of the rice. Refrigerate for at least 2 hours, or until completely cold. (This chill time allows the flavors to develop and infuse through the rice.) If you like, stir in the cream just before serving.

COMMERCY-STYLE MADELEINES

The humble madeleine, with its distinctive shell shape, will always be associated with the French writer Marcel Proust, when he recalled his childhood after tasting a madeleine dipped in tea. But the legend of the madeleine stretches as far back as the 18th century, when a young maid, Madeleine Paulmier, served these little cakes to the exiled king of Poland, who had taken up residence in a castle in the town of Commercy in northeastern France. Besotted with the soft sponge cakes, he named them for the maid and the cakes soon became all the rage with the aristocracy. In this recipe, I have tried my best to stay true to the buttery original made famous in Commercy.

Makes about 16 madeleines

2 oz (60 g) unsalted butter
Pinch of salt
Squeeze of fresh lemon juice
3.5 oz (100 g) beaten eggs (from 2–3 large eggs)
3.5 oz (100 g) sugar
1 tbsp (15 ml) honey
1 tsp vanilla extract
3.5 oz (100 g) all-purpose flour, sifted, plus more for dusting
$^2/_3$ tsp baking powder

MISE EN PLACE

I recommend using a stand mixer to make the batter, but it can also be done by hand. For the bakeware, it's best to use a metal madeleine pan, which is a specialty cake pan with shell-shaped wells. I also recommend using an oven thermometer to ensure a precise baking temperature; otherwise, you run the risk of the madeleines burning or not rising.

In a small saucepan, melt the butter over low heat, then transfer to a bowl. Add the salt and lemon juice to the butter and let it cool until lukewarm.

In the bowl of a stand mixer, combine the eggs, sugar, honey and vanilla. Whisk vigorously for 3 to 4 minutes, or until the mixture thickens and becomes foamy. (This step is very important for the texture of the madeleine.) Add the flour and baking powder and gently mix into a smooth batter.

While the stand mixer is still going, pour in the melted butter in batches, leaving behind the white mass (milk solids) and making sure each batch is fully incorporated before adding the next. When all the butter is incorporated, transfer the batter to a large bowl and cover with plastic wrap, making sure it's in direct contact with the batter to prevent a crust forming on the surface. Let it chill in the fridge for at least 2 hours (overnight is best).

When ready to bake, grease the madeleine pan and dust lightly with flour. Remove the batter from the fridge and fill each madeleine well three-quarters of the way full and no more. Let it sit while you preheat the oven to 350°F (180°C).

Bake the madeleines for 7 to 8 minutes for a light golden result. If you want a darker color and crispier edges, bake at 375°F (190°C) for 6 minutes. When baked, allow them to rest for 10 minutes before unmolding. Enjoy right away or store for up to three days in an airtight container to keep the madeleines from drying out.

TIP

If your egg yolks are on the pale side, use two eggs plus one egg yolk while still respecting the 3½-ounce (100-g) total weight.

VARIATION

Add lemon zest to the batter. For chocolate madeleines, dip the bottom half of the cakes in melted chocolate.

FAMILY-SIZE CRÈME CARAMEL

This delicious custard-based dessert has proven so popular around the world, I don't think there's a cuisine that hasn't fashioned its own version. In France, crème caramel is all about taste and texture. This recipe will make a delicately creamy and silky-smooth crème caramel, but you can adjust the yolk-to-egg-white ratio to create a joyfully wobbly, easy to un-dish dessert that the whole family can dig into.

Serves 6–8

For the Caramel
3.5 oz (100 g) sugar
3 tbsp (45 ml) water

For the Custard
25.3 fl oz (750 ml) whole milk
1 fresh vanilla bean, split in half lengthwise with the seeds scraped
5 large eggs
4 large egg yolks
5.3 oz (150 g) sugar

MISE EN PLACE
This recipe uses the bain-marie (hot water bath) cooking method. You will need a round cake pan at least 9 inches (23 cm) in diameter and 2½ inches (6 cm) deep, and a large baking dish with high edges. Preheat the oven to 300°F (150°C).

VARIATIONS
For a sturdier crème caramel: Use 6 large whole eggs and 3 yolks. For the ultimate delicate and creamy version. Use 4 whole large eggs and 5 yolks.

For the caramel sauce, in a small saucepan, heat the sugar and water over medium heat until the sugar has dissolved. Don't stir or move the pan at this stage. When the mixture starts to bubble, increase the heat to high and cook until the temperature of the sugar reaches 350°F (180°C). This should take between 8 and 10 minutes, but use a food thermometer to monitor the temperature to prevent burning the caramel. When the caramel heats close to 350°F (180°C), it will turn an amber color; swirl gently to achieve an even coloring. As soon as the caramel becomes liquid and starts to smoke, pour it immediately into the cake pan, swirling to evenly coat the bottom.

To make the custard, pour the milk into a large saucepan and add the vanilla bean with the seeds. Bring to a simmer over medium heat. Then break the whole eggs into a large bowl and add the egg yolks and sugar. Using a large whisk, mix gently for 2 minutes, or until most of the sugar has dissolved.

As soon as the milk starts to simmer, turn off the heat and strain half of the milk through a fine-mesh sieve over the egg mixture. Stir gently, then mix in the rest of the milk. To finish, skim away the foam floating on the surface of the custard.

Pour the custard into the caramel-coated cake pan, then place the cake pan in the baking dish. Fill the baking dish with boiling water one-third of the way up the side of the cake pan (avoid dripping any boiling water into the custard) and carefully place on the middle rack of the oven. Bake for 35 minutes.

Remove the crème caramel pan from the baking dish and let it cool before refrigerating. Now, restrain yourself: It's important that the dessert spends at least 12 hours in the fridge to allow the caramel to liquefy and become a silky sauce.

To un-dish, run a knife all around the edges of the cake pan. Place a large, flat plate over the top and quickly flip the pan upside down. Carefully remove the cake pan to let the caramel sauce flow over the sides as the glossy burnt orange surface is revealed (an impressive party trick that never gets old).

CLASSIC FLAMBÉED CRÊPES

Crêpes are beautiful on their own with just a little sugar, chocolate or jam but they can also be used to create an elegant dessert more appropriate for adults than the young ones. The iconic *crêpes flambées* are made *à la minute*, flambéed in a syrup of lemon and orange juice, sugar, Grand Marnier and cognac. Impress guests with this dessert by flambéing the crêpes on a trivet *sur la table* and wait for the applause.

Makes enough to cook 4–6 crêpes

6 or more Crêpes (page 36)

3 tbsp (45 g) unsalted butter, plus extra to finish the sauce

2.5 oz (70 g) sugar

Juice of 2 medium-sized oranges

Juice of 1 small lemon

2 tbsp (30 ml) Grand Marnier

4 tsp (20 ml) cognac

Orange zest and slices, for garnish (optional)

MISE EN PLACE

Make the batter and cook the crêpes according to the recipe on page 36. Allow one or two crêpes per person. I recommend using an 11-inch (28-cm) stainless-steel pan to make the sauce and a gas lighter to flambé the crepes. Juice two medium-sized oranges.

In the pan, combine the butter with the sugar, orange juice, lemon juice and the Grand Marnier over medium heat, mixing well and letting the liquid bubble for 3 minutes, or until it reduces by half. Adjust the heat to low.

Roll the crêpes or fold them into triangles, and place them next to one another in the syrup. Use a spoon to gently baste the crêpes for up to 2 minutes, or until warm and moist. Turn the heat up to high and pour the cognac over the crêpes. Let it heat up for a few seconds, then, with the exhaust fan off, ignite with the gas lighter to flambé. You can bring the pan immediately to the table on a trivet with the flames still flickering to impress. Once the flames die out, stir an extra dab of butter into the sauce and serve immediately. Garnish with orange zest and slices, if using.

ARTISAN CRUSTLESS CHEESECAKE

This Basque-style cheesecake is a regional recipe enjoyed on both sides of the border between France and Spain. Simple to make and easy to love, this rustic-looking dessert is in a league of its own when it comes to cheesecakes. With its moist, creamy texture combined with a delicate taste, it's sure to win over the pickiest of dinner guests.

Serves 4–6

1.1 lb (500 g) cream cheese (Philadelphia brand works best), at room temperature

7 oz (200 g) beaten eggs (from 4 large eggs)

7 oz (200 g) sugar

5 oz (150 ml) heavy cream

2 rounded tbsp (20 g) all-purpose flour

MISE EN PLACE

Grease a 7-inch (18-cm)-diameter springform pan, then line the inside with a large piece of parchment paper. Make sure the paper covers the bottom and hangs over the sides of the pan. You will also need a food processor for this recipe. Preheat the oven to 400°F (200°C).

Cut the cream cheese into medium-sized pieces and pop them into a food processor. Use the pulse function to smooth the cream cheese a little. Add the eggs and process for 1 minute, or until the mixture is smooth with no clumps. If clumps of cheese start to stick to the edges, stop and use a rubber spatula to spoon the cream cheese back into the mixture before continuing to process. Add the sugar, cream and flour and process for 2 to 3 minutes, or until the sugar has completely dissolved. By now, you should have a pale yellow, creamy batter with no lumps. Pour it into the prepared springform pan, taking care that no batter flows over the paper lining.

Bake the cheesecake on the middle shelf of the oven for 40 minutes, or until the top of the cheesecake is dark brown with slightly burnt edges. Don't worry about the burnt patches on top. This is the result you want for that rustic look, and the inside of your cheesecake will be deliciously soft and creamy.

Remove the pan from the oven and rest at room temperature for at least 1 hour until completely cool. You'll notice that the cheesecake deflates a little while cooling down; this is normal. You can serve at room temperature, but it's best enjoyed fridge cold. My tip is to place the cheesecake in the fridge for at least 1 hour before unmolding and serving to eager guests.

EASY CHOCOLATE FONDANT

When the word *chocolate* appears in a French recipe, you know you're in for something good, and it's double the chocolaty goodness with a chocolate fondant. With its moist, crisp exterior and gooey inside that drizzles out when sliced, it makes chocolate cake look like a boring wallflower. A good chocolate fondant can be difficult to get right, but this recipe is foolproof and a breeze to make. Just ensure you use the finest-quality chocolate you can find. Made in just 30 minutes, it's the perfect cake to fix a chocolate craving.

Serves 4

2 large eggs
2 large egg yolks
2.8 oz (80 g) powdered sugar
2.8 oz (80 g) all-purpose flour
1 cup (250 ml) water
3.5 oz (100 g) good-quality dark chocolate (70% cacao)
3.5 oz (100 g) unsalted butter
Pinch of salt
4 tbsp (60 ml) Grand Marnier (optional)

MISE EN PLACE

It's best to use small non-stick pudding molds that are 3 inches (8 cm) in diameter for this recipe, but you can use ramekins. (If you do use ramekins, add a circle of parchment paper to the bottom of each.) Grease and lightly flour each mold, tapping them upside down to remove any excess flour. Preheat the oven to 340°F (170°C).

In a medium-sized glass bowl, beat the whole eggs with the egg yolks. Add the powdered sugar and whisk vigorously for 3 minutes, or until the mixture becomes pale yellow and foamy. Add the flour and gently whisk the ingredients into a smooth batter.

Sit a large glass bowl over a medium-sized saucepan containing the water and bring to a simmer. (Make sure the water doesn't touch the bottom of the bowl.) Add the chocolate and butter to the bowl and sprinkle with the salt. Let soften, untouched, for 3 minutes, then remove the bowl from the heat and use a spatula to delicately mix the ingredients together. Now, fold the chocolate sauce into the bowl with the batter.

Fill each mold with the chocolate batter, leaving a little space at the top. Place the molds on a baking sheet and bake for 10 minutes, or until a light crust forms on top.

Remove from the oven and turn each mold upside down on a small dessert plate to unmold. For a touch of luxury, pour 1 tablespoon of Grand Marnier on top of each fondant just before breaking it open.

NORMANDY APPLE TART WITH CALVADOS

With its elegant fan of caramelized apple slices encased in velvety vanilla custard, this tart is a classic of the Normandy region, which is where you find the best apples and Calvados in France. The interesting twist on the original recipe is to first bake the tart with a layer of apples that have been coated in a Calvados syrup. This method accelerates the cooking of both the apples and the tart base. Pears work just as well in this delicious tart.

Serves 4–6

1 batch All-Purpose Short Crust (sweet version; page 39) or good-quality premade short crust pastry sheet

3–4 Golden Delicious apples or other variety that will hold firm when cooked

2 tbsp (30 g) unsalted butter

3.1 oz (90 g) sugar, divided, plus extra for sprinkling

1 tbsp (15 ml) water

1 tsp fresh lemon juice

1 tbsp (15 ml) Calvados

1 large egg

1 large egg yolk

3.4 fl oz (100 ml) heavy cream

MISE EN PLACE

The ingredients provided here are enough for a 9½-inch (24-cm)-diameter tart pan. If using, make the sweet version of the All-Purpose Short Crust according to the recipe on page 39. Remove the short crust from the fridge at least 30 minutes before rolling it out. Peel, core and halve the apples. Preheat the oven to 425°F (220°C).

Roll out the dough into a circle that's 11 inches (28 cm) in diameter, and use it to line the tart pan. Poke small holes all across the base with a fork. Place the tart base in the freezer to chill.

To make the syrup, in a small saucepan, melt the butter, 1 ounce (30 g) of the sugar and water together over medium heat, stirring occasionally. After about 3 minutes, when the sugar has dissolved and the mixture becomes syrupy, turn off the heat and stir in the lemon juice and Calvados. Give the saucepan a swirl to combine everything, then remove from the heat and set the syrup aside.

Cut each apple half into four small quarters. Remove the tart pan from the freezer and arrange the apples in a spiral to cover the tart base. Use a pastry brush to coat the apples generously with the Calvados syrup, and finish with a sprinkle of sugar on top. Slide the tart onto the middle rack of the oven and bake for 15 minutes, or until the pastry is golden and the apples are lightly caramelized.

Meanwhile, to make the custard, in a medium-sized bowl, whisk together the whole egg, egg yolk, remaining sugar and cream.

After 15 minutes, take the tart out of the oven and pour the custard over the apples. Reduce the oven temperature to 375°F (190°C), return the tart to the oven and bake for 15 minutes, or until the custard has set and becomes lightly colored. Remove from the oven and allow the tart to cool for 15 minutes before serving.

CHOUX NUTS

It's always fascinating to see old things make a comeback. Choux nuts (or Nun's Puff, as they're known in France) are an old-fashioned style of donut made by deep frying choux pastry. They have a texture and consistency similar to classic donuts but are easier and faster to make. Enjoy warm or cold with a generous sprinkle of superfine sugar or filled with jam.

Makes 20 choux nuts

8.5 fl oz (250 ml) whole milk

2 oz (60 g) unsalted butter

1.8 oz (50 g) sugar, plus extra for rolling the choux nuts in

5.3 oz (150 g) all-purpose flour

5.3 oz (150 g) beaten egg (from 2–3 large eggs), at room temperature

1 tsp rum, cognac or Grand Marnier

1 tsp finely grated orange zest

MISE EN PLACE

Set up your deep fryer with about 2 quarts (2 L) of cooking oil and heat the oil to 340°F (170°C). Make a sweet choux pastry using the milk, butter, sugar, flour and egg listed above, following the same process as for the Choux Pastry recipe on page 43. When the choux pastry is ready, mix in the rum and orange zest.

Use a teaspoon to scoop balls of the choux dough and drop them gently into the oil. Fry up to six dough balls at a time to avoid overcrowding the fryer, turning occasionally, for 7 to 8 minutes, or until puffed and golden on all sides. Once the dough balls are frying away in the oil, the key to success is temperature control. Maintaining the temperature at 340°F (170°C) allows the batter to color slowly and puff well for the full donut effect.

Scoop out the puffs to drain and cool on a paper towel–lined plate. To finish, roll in the extra sugar and allow them to cool a little before devouring.

TIP

Ensure the temperature is back to 340°F (170°C) before frying each batch of dough balls.

VARIATION

Add ground cinnamon to the sugar or inject jam into these goodies using a piping bag fitted with an éclair nozzle.

CHOUX CHANTILLY

Here, you get to practice your choux pastry skills and make a classic French dessert at the same time. In France, these homemade choux puffs, filled with swirls of lusciously sweet whipped cream, have been winning people over for centuries. While this basic combination is seriously good, you can take it further by switching the cream for a flavored pastry cream or dipping the tops in melted chocolate and crushed nuts.

Makes 15–20 Choux Chantilly

15–20 choux puffs using a batch of Choux Pastry (page 43)

17 fl oz (500 ml) heavy cream

2 oz (60 g) powdered sugar, plus more to finish

Fresh mint leaves, to garnish (optional)

MISE EN PLACE

I recommend using a stand or hand mixer to whip the cream. You can achieve the same result by hand, but you'll just need to work a little harder. Have a piping bag fitted with a large star tip at the ready. Make the sweet Choux Pastry and cook the choux puffs according to the recipe on page 43. Keep the cream refrigerated for now, and place the bowl you'll be using to whip the cream in the freezer.

When the choux puffs have totally cooled, cut about one-quarter off the top of each puff and set these choux "lids" to the side.

To make the Chantilly cream, take the bowl out of the freezer and pour in the cold cream along with the powdered sugar. Whip the cream on low speed for 1 minute, then raise the speed to medium and continue whipping until visible streaks start to form. Finish the job by hand to avoid overwhipping the cream: Grab a whisk and continue to whip until the cream is firm.

Scoop the Chantilly cream into the piping bag and fill each choux puff first with a squeeze of cream followed by a generous swirl on top. Place the choux lids over the top and plant a mint leaf in the cream, if using. Sprinkle with powdered sugar before serving.

PARISIAN CUSTARD TART

Everyone in France nurses a little fondness for the Parisian flan, or *flan pâtissier*. This simple custard tart can be found in every French boulangerie and patisserie, with a pastry cream texture that ranges from rubbery to velvety smooth. In French restaurants, chefs are now taking the flan up a notch by experimenting with dark sugars and exotic vanilla flavors. For home cooking, I've aimed to keep the recipe as simple and delicious as possible without sacrificing taste and texture. We'll use a fresh vanilla bean, whole milk, cream and short crust for a deliciously creamy flan with a buttery, flaky crust.

Serves 4

1 batch All-Purpose Short Crust (page 39) or 1 premade puff pastry sheet

15.2 fl oz (450 ml) whole milk

5 fl oz (150 ml) heavy cream

1 fresh vanilla pod, split in half lengthwise with the seeds scraped

1 large egg

1 large egg yolk

4.5 oz (130 g) sugar

1.8 oz (50 g) cornstarch

2 tbsp (30 g) salted butter

1 tbsp (15 ml) pure maple syrup, to glaze (optional)

MISE EN PLACE

If using, make the All-Purpose Short Crust according to the directions on page 39. Grease the inside of an 8-inch (20-cm)-diameter round springform cake pan, dust lightly with flour and then line it with the pastry so that it covers the bottom and the sides. Keep the cake pan in the freezer until the pastry is rock solid. Preheat the oven to 340°F (170°C).

In a large saucepan, combine the milk and cream and place over medium heat. Add the vanilla pod and bring the mixture to a simmer, stirring from time to time.

Meanwhile, in a large bowl, whisk together the egg, egg yolk and sugar until the mixture becomes a pale-yellow color, then gently blend in the cornstarch.

As soon as the milk mixture starts to simmer, turn off the heat and discard the vanilla pod. Strain half of the milk mixture through a sieve into the egg mixture and whisk to combine before pouring in the rest. Give the custard a gentle stir, taking care not to whisk too hard, to prevent it becoming too foamy.

Pour the custard into the same saucepan used to heat the milk and place over medium heat. Whisk constantly, but gently, for 3 to 5 minutes, or until the custard thickens and starts to boil. When it does, adjust the heat to low and continue to cook for 2 minutes, then turn off the heat and incorporate the butter.

Remove the cake pan from the freezer and scrape the warm pastry cream into the pastry casing, smoothing evenly with a spatula. Place the cake pan on the middle shelf of the oven and bake for 45 minutes, or until the surface of the flan is golden with large brown patches. Remove from the oven and allow the flan to cool at room temperature before placing it in the fridge for at least 3 hours, ideally overnight. The flan must be completely cold before it's unmolded. Brush the top of the flan with some maple syrup (if using) to provide some shine before serving.

NOTE
Double the ingredients for a 10-inch (25-cm)-diameter springform cake pan.

PETIT RASPBERRY MILLE-FEUILLE

Known outside of France as vanilla slice, this lovely dessert is about two things: thin slabs of pastry cream sandwiched between layers of buttery puff pastry. This home-friendly version is made with a silky pastry cream flavored with a hint of liquor, encased in two caramelized pastry sheets. A layer of fresh raspberries is added for fruitiness and a pop of color.

Serves 4–6

1 premade butter puff pastry sheet

1 batch Pastry Cream (page 40)

2½ fl oz (75 ml) heavy cream

1.4 oz (40 g) superfine sugar

1 tbsp (15 ml) white rum

7 oz (200 g) fresh raspberries

2½ tbsp (20 g) powdered sugar, to garnish

MISE EN PLACE

Make sure the puff pastry sheet is defrosted, but fridge-cold, before ready to use. Make the Pastry Cream according to the recipe on page 40. Chill in the fridge for at least 1 hour. Keep the heavy cream refrigerated for now, and place the bowl you'll be using to whip the heavy cream in the freezer. Preheat the oven to 400°F (200°C). Line a baking sheet with parchment paper.

Place the cold pastry sheet on the baking sheet and use a fork to prick holes all over the pastry. Cover the pastry sheet with another piece of parchment paper, then place a second baking sheet on top. Transfer to the oven and place a large baking dish on top to act as a weight, to prevent the puff pastry from rising too much. Bake for 15 minutes, then remove the weight, baking sheet and top sheet of parchment paper and sprinkle the pastry with the superfine sugar. Continue to bake for 10 to 15 minutes, or until golden and lightly caramelized. When done, remove from the oven and let the pastry sheet cool on a cooling rack while you make the filling.

Remove the pastry cream from the fridge, and set it aside while you whip the heavy cream. Use the bowl kept chilled in the freezer to whip the heavy cream until it becomes just firm. Now add the rum to the pastry cream and whisk vigorously to get it back to a creamy consistency, and then fold in the whipped cream.

To assemble the mille-feuilles, use a serrated cake knife to carefully slice the caramelized pastry sheet into small rectangles. (The standard size is 2 x 4 inches [5 x 10 cm].) Start with one rectangle of puff pastry, caramel side up, as the base and spread a layer of cream, 1-inch (2.5-cm) thick, on top. Next, line up two rows of four raspberries next to each other on top and cover the raspberries with a second layer of pastry cream. Cover with another puff pastry rectangle to finish. Repeat to assemble each piece.

Tidy the sides of the mille-feuilles with a spatula and dust the tops with the powdered sugar. Chill in the fridge for at least 1 hour before serving.

TIP

Be aware that puff pastry is tricky to slice. Cutting the puff pastry into rectangles before building the mille-feuilles makes assembly and presentation much simpler.

TRADITIONAL BASQUE CAKE WITH BLACK CHERRY JAM

This traditional cake, a regional specialty from the northern Basque region in France, has a reputation for being both simple and delicious. It's a type of sweet pie with a filling of pastry cream or cherry jam sandwiched between two layers of a melt-in-your-mouth cookie-like crust. I like the fast and fuss-free version that just uses black cherry jam filling, but you can replace this with Pastry Cream (page 40) or include both. This versatile recipe is still made in homes all around the Basque country, enjoyed warm or cold, at any time of the day.

Serves 6

9.7 oz (275 g) all-purpose flour, plus more for dusting

7 oz (200 g) superfine sugar

1 tbsp (15 g) vanilla sugar (see page 9)

2 pinches of salt

2 rounded tsp (10 g) baking powder

1 tsp grated lemon zest

6.2 oz (175 g) unsalted butter, cut into small cubes

1 large egg

2 large egg yolks

12 oz (350 g) black cherry jam (or preserves)

Egg wash (1 egg yolk mixed with 1 tsp water)

MISE EN PLACE

For the bakeware, I used a greased 9½-inch (24-cm)-diameter low-sided pie dish, but you can also use a cake or tart pan.

In a large bowl, combine the flour, sugars, salt, baking powder and lemon zest and mix well. Add the butter and work the ingredients together with your fingers until the mixture becomes crumbly, and then use a spatula to mix in the egg and egg yolks until a dough begins to form. Knead the dough a little with your hands, and dust with some flour if it's too sticky. Place the dough on a clean, flour-dusted kitchen counter and roll it into a ball.

Divide the dough into two pieces, one larger than the other (about 60/40 of the total weight). Use your hands to flatten both pieces slightly into a rough circle and wrap separately in plastic wrap. Rest the dough in the fridge for 2 hours. (Make sure you remove the dough from the fridge 30 minutes before you start to work with it so that it's soft and malleable.) Lightly dust the base and sides of the greased pie dish with flour, turning over the pan and tapping it to remove any excess.

Use a rolling pin to roll out the larger piece of dough into a circle that's 10 inches (25 cm) in diameter, and line the pie dish with the edges of the dough loose around the sides of the dish. Place the jam in the center and smooth evenly all the way to the edges, and then fold the sides of the dough 1¼ inches (3 cm) inward over the jam.

Roll the second piece of dough to create a smaller circle, 9 inches (23 cm) in diameter, and place it neatly on top. Use your finger or the back of a fork to neatly tuck the edges of the dough toward the inside of the dish, applying pressure all around the outer perimeter to seal the pieces of dough together.

Leave the cake to chill in the fridge while you preheat the oven to 340°F (170°C). Remove the cake from the fridge after 15 minutes and brush the surface of the cake with the egg wash, then use a fork to score a faint crisscross pattern. Bake for 40 to 45 minutes, or until golden. Remove the cake from the oven and allow it to cool completely before unmolding. The cake will keep for up to 3 days at room temperature or in the fridge.

ALMOND CREAM PITHIVIER

Also known as the king cake, this sweet pie of almond cream sandwiched in a warm butter puff pastry is traditionally enjoyed during Epiphany in France. The ritual is to hide a *fève* (little figurine) inside the frangipane cream and serve the cake cut into slices covered with a clean tea towel. The lucky person who draws the slice with the *fève* is crowned king or queen and gets to wear a cardboard crown for the night. This is my no-fuss recipe that uses premade puff pastry and an almond filling. You can also add pastry cream to the almond paste for a true *crème frangipane*.

Makes 1 (10" [25-cm])-diameter cake

7 oz (200 g) Pastry Cream (optional, page 40)

2 rolls or sheets premade butter puff pastry

7 oz (200 g) unsalted butter

7 oz (200 g) sugar

7 oz (200 g) eggs (from 4 large eggs), at room temperature

7 oz (200 g) almond meal

1 tbsp (8 g) all-purpose flour

1 tbsp (15 ml) white or dark rum

2 drops of bitter almond extract

Egg wash (1 egg yolk mixed with 1 tsp water)

MISE EN PLACE

If using, make the Pastry Cream according to the recipe on page 40. Ensure all ingredients are at room temperature and the puff pastry is defrosted and ready in the fridge. Cut the butter into small cubes and let soften until it can be spread effortlessly with a spoon. Line a baking sheet with parchment paper.

To make the almond paste, place the soft butter cubes in a large bowl and use a spatula to flatten them into a smooth paste. Add the sugar and whisk until fully combined.

In a separate small bowl, beat the eggs, then pour one-quarter of the eggs at a time into the butter mixture, whisking vigorously until fully incorporated before adding the next portion. Once all the egg is incorporated, add the almond meal and flour, then whisk again until the ingredients form a thick paste. Add the rum and carefully tap 2 drops of almond extract in (no more, otherwise the flavor will be too strong). If using pastry cream, mix it with the almond cream now. When ready, chill the almond cream in the fridge while you prepare the puff pastry.

Preheat the oven to 400°F (200°C).

To make the crust, use a large bowl as a guide to cut a circle that's 10 inches [25 cm] in diameter, or smaller, from each puff pastry sheet. Keep one pastry circle in the fridge and use the other to start assembling the pithivier.

Place the pastry circle on the baking sheet and spoon the almond cream in the center. Spread the almond cream evenly with a palette knife to a 1½-inch (4-cm) thickness, leaving a 1½-inch (4-cm) margin around the edges.

Brush all around the edges of the pastry with the egg wash, then remove the second pastry circle from the fridge and place it neatly on top. Use your hands to seal the pastry circles together by applying light pressure all around the edges. Trim any untidy bits from around the pithivier, then use the back of a knife to make inward indentations around the edges to completely seal the pastry circles together. (This prevents any leakage during baking.)

NOTE

There's no rule that says a pie must be a circular shape. You can use the original square or rectangle pastry sheets to make this cake.

If using, add the figurine with the almond cream before placing the second pastry circle on top.

Fully coat the top of the pithivier with egg wash, then chill for 30 minutes. Then, add a second layer of egg wash and channel your inner artist to decorate the top, making lines or shapes using the back of a knife. Finish by cutting a small hole in the center to allow steam to escape during baking. Bake for 40 minutes, or until well puffed and golden. Remove from the oven and allow the pie to cool on a cooling rack for 15 minutes before you attempt to slice it and serve.

MÈRE BRAZIER'S FLOATING ISLAND DESSERT

This decadent dessert delivers a small taste of the remarkable legacy of Eugénie Brazier, so gifted with culinary skills that she became the star of the *Mères de France* movement in the 1900s. In 1933, she was the first woman to be awarded the title of "chef," and her small restaurant was given the rare accolade of three Michelin stars. With a poached meringue dappled with pink praline floating on a sea of vanilla custard, her version of the floating island dessert dazzles the eye. This indulgent dessert will bring a wow factor to special occasions.

Serves 4–6

For the Custard
17 fl oz (500 ml) whole milk

1 vanilla bean, split in half lengthwise with the seeds scraped

5.3 oz (150 g) sugar

4 large egg yolks

For the Meringue
4 large egg whites

Small pinch of salt

½ tsp fresh lemon juice

1.8 oz (50 g) sugar

2 rounded tbsp (20 g) crushed pink praline, plus more to garnish

1 rounded tbsp (10 g) shaved toasted almonds, to garnish

MISE EN PLACE
This recipe requires a lidded pudding mold that is approximately 6 inches (15 cm) diameter. You will also need a stand mixer to make the meringue and a food thermometer for the caramel. Preheat the oven to 285°F (140°C).

Start by making the vanilla custard: In a large saucepan, combine the milk and vanilla bean and bring to a light boil over medium heat.

While the milk is warming up, in a large bowl, vigorously whisk the sugar and egg yolks until smooth. Keep an eye on the milk, and as soon as it simmers, strain half of it through a fine-mesh sieve over the egg mixture, whisking gently to combine. Then, mix the rest of the milk in, and pour the custard back into the same saucepan.

Heat the custard over medium heat, stirring constantly with a wooden spoon, until it reaches 180°F (83°C) or is thick enough to coat the back of the spoon. (Stir constantly to prevent the egg yolk from curdling at the bottom of the pan.) Filter through a sieve into a bowl and let it cool at room temperature before storing in the fridge for at least 2 hours, or until completely cold.

When the custard is cold, make the meringue. In the bowl of a stand mixer, whisk the egg whites with the salt and lemon juice on high speed for 3 minutes until they double in volume, then reduce the speed to medium and add the sugar a little at a time. Flick the speed to high again and continue to whisk for up to 3 minutes until you have a glossy and firm meringue. Stop the mixer and use a spatula to fold in the crushed pink praline.

To poach the meringue, brush the inside of the pudding mold with cooking oil, then cut a circle of parchment paper to fit the bottom of the mold. (This will prevent the meringue from sticking to the mold when cooked.) Spoon the meringue into the pudding mold, cover with parchment paper, then pop on the lid before placing it into a baking dish. Fill the dish with boiling water halfway up the sides of the pudding mold, then bake for 15 to 20 minutes maximum, until the meringue is firm. When cooked, carefully unmold the meringue onto a flat plate, removing the parchment paper.

(continued)

For the Caramel

1.8 oz (50 g) sugar

1 tbsp (15 ml) water

To assemble the dessert, pour the cold custard into a serving dish with high edges and delicately slide the poached meringue into the middle.

To make the caramel, in a saucepan, combine the sugar and water and bring to a boil. Cook until the liquid turns an amber color, then check the temperature with a food thermometer. When the temperature hits 350°F (180°C) and the caramel starts to smoke, it's ready. Immediately drizzle the caramel all over the meringue and sprinkle with crushed praline and the toasted almonds.

Well done—Mère Brazier would be proud. Your glorious floating island is ready to be eaten.

NOTE

Pink praline are almonds with a pink sugar coating. They can be sourced from online gourmet food stores or professional baking stores.

ICE CREAM AND MERINGUE VACHERIN
WITH BERRIES

If you're looking to impress with an elegant dessert without the skills of a pastry chef, this recipe is for you. Vacherin is a classy French dessert made with layers of ice cream sandwiched between meringue and decorated with whipped cream and a stack of berries. Not only does it look as if it could be served as part of a Gatsby-esque buffet, but it also tastes divine. I use two different flavors of ice cream, but you can get away with just vanilla. Don't let the number of steps deter you; while it takes a little patience, this dessert is not too difficult and makes an impressive masterpiece for special occasions.

Serve 6

2 batches Traditional French Meringue (page 35)
1 qt (1 L) vanilla ice cream
1 qt (1 L) raspberry ice cream
2 batches Mascarpone Whipped Cream (page 33)
7 oz (200 g) fresh mixed berries

MISE EN PLACE

You will need a cake ring that is 8 inches (20 cm) in diameter and 4 inches (10 cm) high, along with three disposable piping bags, a medium-sized straight tip and a large star tip. Make the Traditional French Meringue according to the recipe on page 35 and double the ingredients to make a double batch. Preheat the oven to 190°F (90°C).

Cover two baking sheets with parchment paper and use a pencil to trace around the cake ring, drawing two circles separated by a few inches on one of the sheets. When done, flip the parchment paper over to avoid getting pencil marks on your meringue.

To create the meringue disks, fit a piping bag with the straight tip and fill it with the meringue. Pipe a spiral over each of the circles, starting from the center and working outward until just outside the perimeter of the circle. When both spirals are done, set aside.

To make the decorative elements for the top of the vacherin, take a second piping bag fitted with a star tip and fill it with meringue. Pipe eight or more star shapes or swirls onto the second prepared baking sheet. When done, bake the meringue in the oven for 2 hours, then allow to dry at room temperature for 1 hour. Reserve the meringue on a plate at room temperature until needed in the recipe.

To build the vacherin, pull the ice cream out of the freezer and let it soften a little in the fridge until it becomes malleable. On a flat surface, place a meringue disk on a silicone mat or parchment paper. Carefully position the cake ring over the meringue, then press down firmly so that the cake ring cuts through neatly. Gently remove the meringue disk from the cake ring and repeat, using the second disk, but this time leave the disk attached at the bottom of the cake ring. (This will be the base of the vacherin, and the other disk will be used for the top.)

Transfer the meringue-based cake ring to a cake board, then carefully and quickly fill it with the vanilla and raspberry ice cream, leaving a 1-inch (2.5 cm) space at the top. Slot in the second meringue disk on top and press down very gently so that the disk sticks to the ice cream. Slide this ice cream sandwich onto a plate and freeze overnight until rock solid.

(continued)

The next day, remove the vacherin from the freezer and let it sit at room temperature for a few minutes before gently extracting it from the ring. Pop it back in the freezer while you make the Mascarpone Whipped Cream. Make the Mascarpone Whipped Cream according to the recipe on page 33 by doubling the ingredients for a double batch.

Spoon half of the Mascarpone Whipped Cream into a piping bag fitted with a star tip, leaving the rest in the bowl. Keep the piping bag chilled in the fridge for now.

Remove the vacherin from the freezer and use a palette knife to apply a thin, smooth layer of Mascarpone Whipped Cream from the bowl all around the sides and on top. When done, rest the vacherin in the freezer again for at least 1 hour.

Have a plan of action to decorate the vacherin and be ready to work quickly, because the ice cream will melt fast. Remove the vacherin from the freezer and use the piping bag of mascarpone whipped cream to decorate the top with swirls, lines or dots and also arrange the meringue shapes. Finish by planting the berries decoratively for a pop of color and serve immediately

As you can imagine, you can't leave this iced dessert on the table for long before it starts to melt. To slice easily, dip a knife in warm water, then wipe dry with a clean tea towel before cutting each slice. To go the extra mile, serve with a red fruit coulis.

ACKNOWLEDGMENTS

We must begin by thanking each other for maintaining focus while we poured our heart and soul into creating our first book. It really has been a roller-coaster ride while we lived, breathed (and ate) the content of this book for almost a year. Somehow, we both managed to keep the other sane (but the odd glass of pinot noir with cheese also helped).

Thanks to the team at Page Street Publishing and our editor, Aïcha. Your faith in this project has been unwavering, and we appreciate your prompt answering of our endless questions without any hint of exasperation.

To our community of producers in the southwest of Victoria, thank you for supplying us with fresh, sustainably grown produce. A dish is only the sum of its parts, and your beautiful produce, grown and sourced with love, made our dishes shine: Merri Banks Market Garden, Volcano Produce, Stokes River Chicken, Mount Zero Olives, Allfresh Seafood, Symons Organic Dairy and Schulz Organic Dairy. Thank you to Fenn Food & Wine Store for meeting the odd specialty ingredient request and Amanda for the farm eggs.

To Jo, Rocky and Amy for the extended loan of various plates, cutlery and food-styling props. And Robin and Dennis for the photo-editing tips.

To all our friends and family who have supported us from the very beginning and have never been short of words of encouragement. To all our nieces and nephews, the future of French home cooking.

To Gary and Evelyn, for your enthusiasm to taste test recipes in their various stages of development (and for letting us raid your garden for the kilos of parsley it took to make this book).

Finally, to every follower, subscriber and student, a big *merci* goes to you. The French Cooking Academy wouldn't be what it is today without you. Your support, encouragement and enthusiasm have helped keep the passion for homestyle French cooking alive all these years.

Stephane and Kate are the husband-and-wife duo who created the widely celebrated French Cooking Academy online cooking school and YouTube channel of the same name. Reaching millions of people every year, they aim to demystify French cooking, with simple tips, basic recipes and step-by-step tutorials amateur cooks can use to better their skills. Stephane is a self-taught cook who grew up in Fontainebleau, France, with a natural teaching style and no-fuss approach to French cooking that some followers have likened to Julia Child. Stephane has appeared on SBS television and radio, and French Cooking Academy has been featured in print and online, including *France-Ameriques*, Air Canada's *enRoute* and *My French Country Home Magazine*. Stephane and Kate now live in regional Victoria, Australia, where they enjoy discovering local food producers, growing their own ingredients and creating boutique courses that teach the art of French cooking.

INDEX

A

Aioli Platter, Grand, 60–61

All-Purpose Short Crust, 39

Almond Cream Pithivier, 210–211

appetizers

    Baked Eggs à la Florentine, 94

    Baked Eggs with Tomato, Capers and Croutons, 51

    Caramelized Onion and Bacon Quiche, 59

    Classic Salmon Tartare, 93

    Creamy Ham and Cheese Feuilleté, 98

    Eggs Mimosa, 48

    Gougères, 55

    Grand Aioli Platter, 60–61

    Greek-Style Mushrooms, 52

    Mackerel Escabèche, 97

    Tapenade, 47

    Tomato and Mustard Feuilleté, 56

    Twice-Baked Cheese and Ham Soufflé with Gourmet Mushrooms, 100–101

Apple Tart with Calvados, Normandy, 199

Artisan Crustless Cheesecake, 195

Asparagus with Mousseline Sauce, 82

B

Bacon Quiche, Caramelized Onion and, 59

Baked Coconut Treats, 183

Baked Eggs à la Florentine, 94

Baked Eggs with Tomato, Capers and Croutons, 51

Baked Lamb Chops "Champvallon" with Onions and Potatoes, 128

Basque-Style Sautéed Courgettes, 177

beans (green), in Lyonnaise Sautéed Green Beans, 162

beans (white), in Brittany White Beans, 174

Béarnaise, Easy, 24

Beaujolais-Style Chicken, 127

Béchamel, Classic, 23

beef, in Red Wine Beef Ragout Dauphinoise, 137

Beef Daube with Spring Carrots, 112

Beef in Dark Belgian Beer, Slow-Cooked, 133

beer, in Slow-Cooked Beef in Dark Belgian Beer, 133

berries, in Ice Cream and Meringue Vacherin with Berries, 215–217

Bistro Fish Filets with Sautéed Potatoes, 150

Bistro Steak and Fries with Herb Butter, 107

Black Cherry Jam, Traditional Basque Cake with, 208

Braised Chicken in Tarragon Sauce, 123

Braised Chicken the Corsican Way, 134

Braised Lamb Shanks in Port Wine, 120

Breaded Fish Filets with Tartare Sauce, 146

Brittany White Beans, 174

Brown Chicken Stock, 13

Burgundy-Style Red Wine Sauce, 32

Burgundy-Style Vinaigrette, 17–18

butter, 8

Butter, Steak Herb, 21

C

cakes

    Almond Cream Pithivier, 210–211

    Commercy-Style Madeleines, 188

    Easy Chocolate Fondant, 196

    Petit Raspberry Mille-Feuille, 207

    Traditional Basque Cake with Black Cherry Jam, 208

Calvados, Creamy Sautéed Chicken with Cider and, 141

Calvados, Normandy Apple Tart with, 199

Calvados Sauce, Normandy-Style Pork Chops with Cider and, 115

Caramelized Onion and Bacon Quiche, 59

carrots

    Beef Daube with Spring Carrots, 112

    Crécy Carrot Soup, 86

    Parisian Carrot Salad, 77

Cauliflower Gratin, Classic, 165

Celeriac Salad with Homemade Mayonnaise, 81

Chantilly, Choux, 203

cheese
>Artisan Crustless Cheesecake, 195
>Classic Cauliflower Gratin, 165
>Creamy Ham and Cheese Feuilleté, 98
>Gougères, 55
>Twice-Baked Cheese and Ham Soufflé with Gourmet Mushrooms, 100–101
>Warm Goat Cheese Salad, 69

chicken
>Beaujolais-Style Chicken, 127
>Braised Chicken in Tarragon Sauce, 123
>Braised Chicken the Corsican Way, 134
>Brown Chicken Stock, 13
>Chicken Chasseur, 119
>Chicken Velouté Sauce, 27
>Creamy Sautéed Chicken with Cider and Calvados, 141
>Homestyle Demi-Glace, 15
>Market Rotisserie Chicken with Potato and Tomato Garnish, 104–105
>My Signature Chicken Soup, 90
>Poulet Sauté Alice, 138
>Seared Chicken Breasts in Creamy Mushroom Sauce, 111
>White Chicken Stock, 12

Chocolate Fondant, Easy, 196

Choux Chantilly, 203

Choux Nuts, 200

Choux Pastry, 43

Cider and Calvados, Creamy Sautéed Chicken with, 141

Cider and Calvados Sauce, Normandy-Style Pork Chops with, 115

Classic Béchamel, 23

Classic Cauliflower Gratin, 165

Classic Flambéed Crêpes, 192

Classic French Dressings, 17–18

Classic Parisian Salad, 70

Classic Salmon Tartare, 93

Coconut Treats, Baked, 183

Commercy-Style Madeleines, 188

cooking tips, 8–9

Corn Velouté, Creamy, 89

Courgettes, Basque-Style Sautéed, 177

cream, 8

Creamy Corn Velouté, 89

Creamy Garlic Vinaigrette, 18

Creamy Ham and Cheese Feuilleté, 98

Creamy Sautéed Chicken with Cider and Calvados, 141

Crécy Carrot Soup, 86

Crème Caramel, Family-Size, 191

Crêpes, 36

Crêpes, Classic Flambéed, 192

croutons, in Baked Eggs with Tomato, Capers and Croutons, 51

Crust, All-Purpose Short, 39

Cucumbers in Cream Dressing, 74

Custard Tart, Parisian, 204

D

Demi-Glace, Homestyle, 15

Dijon mustard, in Mustard Vinaigrette, 17–18

dips
>Aioli, 60
>Tapenade, 47

donuts, Choux Nuts, 200

dressings. See vinaigrettes

Duchess Potatoes, 170

Duck Fat, Sautéed Potatoes in, 166

E

Easy Béarnaise, 24

Easy Chocolate Fondant, 196

eggs
>Baked Eggs à la Florentine, 94
>Baked Eggs with Tomato, Capers and Croutons, 51
>Eggs Mimosa, 48
>Twice-Baked Cheese and Ham Soufflé with Gourmet Mushrooms, 100–101

Escabèche, Mackerel, 97

F

Family-Size Crème Caramel, 191

Farmhouse Lentil Salad, 66

Feuilleté, Creamy Ham and Cheese, 98

Feuilleté, Tomato and Mustard, 56

fish. See seafood

Floating Island Dessert, Mère Brazier's, 213–214

flour, toasting, 9

Fondant, Easy Chocolate, 196

French Garden Peas with a Twist, 178

French Onion Soup with Port Wine, 85

French-Style Pilaf Rice, 161

Fresh Herb Vinaigrette, 17–18

G

Garden-Fresh Tomato Sauce, 29

garlic, in Grand Aioli Platter, 60–61

Garlic Vinaigrette, Creamy, 17–18

Gherkin Sauce, Pork Chops with Mustard and, 130

Gougères, 55

Grand Aioli Platter, 60–61

Grand Marnier, Vanilla Rice Pudding with Raisins and, 187

Greek-Style Mushrooms, 52

Green Beans, Lyonnaise Sautéed, 162

H

ham, in Twice-Baked Cheese and Ham Soufflé with Gourmet Mushrooms, 100–101

Ham and Cheese Feuilleté, Creamy, 98

Herb Vinaigrette, Fresh, 17–18

Hollandaise, No-Fuss, 26

Homemade Mayonnaise, 22

Homestyle Demi-Glace, 15

hors d'oeuvres. *See* appetizers

I

Ice Cream and Meringue Vacherin with Berries, 215–217

L

Lamb Chops "Champvallon" with Onions and Potatoes, Baked, 128

Lamb Shanks in Port Wine, Braised, 120

leeks, in Spring Leeks with Vinaigrette, 78

Lemon and Rosemary Vinaigrette, 17–18

Lentil Salad, Farmhouse, 66

Lyonnaise Bistro Salad, 65

Lyonnaise Sautéed Green Beans, 162

M

Macarons, Old-Fashioned, 184

Mackerel Escabèche, 97

Madeleines, Commercy-Style, 188

Maître d' Steak Tartare, 108

Marinière Mussels with Pommes Frites, 145

Market Rotisserie Chicken with Potato and Tomato Garnish, 104–105

Mascarpone Whipped Cream, 33

Mayonnaise, Homemade, 22

measurements, 8

Mère Brazier's Floating Island Dessert, 213–214

Meringue, Traditional French, 35

Mille-Feuille, Petit Raspberry, 207

mise en place, 8

Morel Mushroom Sauce with Madeira Wine, 30

Mornay sauce, 23

Mousseline sauce, 26

mushrooms
Chicken Chasseur, 119
Greek-Style Mushrooms, 52
Morel Mushroom Sauce with Madeira Wine, 30
Potato Gratin with Mushrooms, 169
Seared Chicken Breasts in Creamy Mushroom Sauce, 111
Twice-Baked Cheese and Ham Soufflé with Gourmet Mushrooms, 100–101

mussels, in Marinière Mussels with Pommes Frites, 145

Mustard and Gherkin Sauce, Pork Chops with, 130

Mustard Feuilleté, Tomato and, 56

Mustard Vinaigrette, 17–18

My Signature Chicken Soup, 90

N

Niçoise Salad, 73

No-Fuss Hollandaise, 26

Normandy Apple Tart with Calvados, 199

Normandy-Style Pork Chops with Cider and Calvados Sauce, 115

O

oils, 17

Old-Fashioned Macarons, 184

olives, in Tapenade, 47

Onion and Bacon Quiche, Caramelized, 59

onions, in French Onion Soup with Port Wine, 85

Oven-Baked Fish with White Vermouth à la Minute, 157

oven temperatures, 8

P

Panfried Steak with Red Wine Sauce, 124

Parisian Carrot Salad, 77

Parisian Custard Tart, 204

Pastry, Choux, 43

Pastry Cream, 40

peas, in French Garden Peas with a Twist, 178

peppercorns, in Steak au Poivre, 116

Petit Raspberry Mille-Feuille, 207

Pilaf Rice, French-Style, 161

Pithivier, Almond Cream, 210–211

Poached Fish in Tomato and Vermouth Sauce, 149

Pork Chops with Cider and Calvados Sauce, Normandy-Style, 115

Pork Chops with Mustard and Gherkin Sauce, 130

potatoes

Baked Lamb Chops "Champvallon" with Onions and Potatoes, 128

Bistro Fish Filets with Sautéed Potatoes, 150

Bistro Steak and Fries with Herb Butter, 107

Duchess Potatoes, 170

Marinière Mussels with Pommes Frites, 145

Market Rotisserie Chicken with Potato and Tomato Garnish, 104–105

Potato Gratin with Mushrooms, 169

Potatoes Boulangère, 173

Sautéed Potatoes in Duck Fat, 166

Poulet Sauté Alice, 138

pudding, Vanilla Rice Pudding with Raisins and Grand Marnier, 187

Q

Quiche, Caramelized Onion and Bacon, 59

Quick Seafood Stock, 16

R

Ragout Dauphinoise, Red Wine Beef, 137

raisins, in Vanilla Rice Pudding with Raisins and Grand Marnier, 187

Raspberry Mille-Feuille, Petit, 207

Red Wine Beef Ragout Dauphinoise, 137

Rice, French-Style Pilaf, 161

rice, in Vanilla Rice Pudding with Raisins and Grand Marnier, 187

Roquefort (Blue Cheese) Vinaigrette, 17–18

Rosemary Vinaigrette, Lemon and, 17–18

S

Saffron Velouté Sauce, Fish with, 154

salads

Asparagus with Mousseline Sauce, 82

Celeriac Salad with Homemade Mayonnaise, 81

Classic Parisian Salad, 70

Cucumbers in Cream Dressing, 74

Farmhouse Lentil Salad, 66

Lyonnaise Bistro Salad, 65

Niçoise Salad, 73

Parisian Carrot Salad, 77

Spring Leeks with Vinaigrette, 70

Warm Goat Cheese Salad, 69

Salmon Tartare, Classic, 93

salt, seasoning with, 9

sauces

Burgundy-Style Red Wine Sauce, 32

Chicken Velouté Sauce, 27

Classic Béchamel, 23

Easy Béarnaise, 24

Garden-Fresh Tomato Sauce, 29

Morel Mushroom Sauce with Madeira Wine, 30

Mornay sauce, 23

Mousseline sauce, 26

No-Fuss Hollandaise, 26

tartare sauce, 146

Sautéed Potatoes in Duck Fat, 166

scallops, in Fish and Scallops à la Mornay, 153

seafood

Bistro Fish Filets with Sautéed Potatoes, 150

Breaded Fish Filets with Tartare Sauce, 146

Classic Salmon Tartare, 93

Fish and Scallops à la Mornay, 153

Fish with Saffron Velouté Sauce, 154

Grand Aioli Platter, 60–61

Mackerel Escabèche, 97

Marinière Mussels with Pommes Frites, 145

Niçoise Salad, 73

Oven-Baked Fish with White Vermouth à la Minute, 157

Poached Fish in Tomato and Vermouth Sauce, 149

Quick Seafood Stock, 16

Seared Chicken Breasts in Creamy Mushroom Sauce, 111

Slow-Cooked Beef in Dark Belgian Beer, 133

snacks. *See* appetizers

Soufflé with Gourmet Mushrooms, Twice-Baked Cheese and Ham, 100–101

soups
Creamy Corn Velouté, 89
Crécy Carrot Soup, 86
French Onion Soup with Port Wine, 85
My Signature Chicken Soup, 90

spinach, in Baked Eggs à la Florentine, 94

Spring Leeks with Vinaigrette, 78

Steak Herb Butter, 21

steaks
Bistro Steak and Fries with Herb Butter, 107
Maître d' Steak Tartare, 108
Panfried Steak with Red Wine Sauce, 124
Steak au Poivre, 116

stock, 9
Brown Chicken Stock, 13
Homestyle Demi-Glace, 15
Quick Seafood Stock, 16
White Chicken Stock, 12

T

Tapenade, 47

Tarragon Sauce, Braised Chicken in, 123

tart, Normandy Apple Tart with Calvados, 199

Tart, Parisian Custard, 204

Tartare, Classic Salmon, 93

Tartare, Maître d' Steak, 108

Tartare Sauce, Breaded Fish Filets with, 146

tips, cooking, 8–9

toasting flour, 9

Tomato, Capers and Croutons, Baked Eggs with, 51

Tomato and Mustard Feuilleté, 56

Tomato and Vermouth Sauce, Poached Fish in, 149

Tomato Sauce, Garden-Fresh, 29

Traditional Basque Cake with Black Cherry Jam, 208

Traditional French Meringue, 35

Traditional Vinaigrette, 17–18

tuna, in Niçoise Salad, 73

Twice-Baked Cheese and Ham Soufflé with Gourmet Mushrooms, 100–101

V

vacherin, Ice Cream and Meringue Vacherin with Berries, 215–217

Vanilla Rice Pudding with Raisins and Grand Marnier, 187

vanilla sugar, 9

Velouté, Creamy Corn, 89

Velouté Sauce, Chicken, 27

Velouté Sauce, Fish with Saffron, 154

vinaigrettes, 17–18

vinegar, 17

W

Warm Goat Cheese Salad, 69

Whipped Cream, Mascarpone, 33

white beans, in Brittany White Beans, 174

White Chicken Stock, 12

wine
Beaujolais-Style Chicken, 127
Burgundy-Style Red Wine Sauce, 32
Red Wine Beef Ragout Dauphinoise, 137

Z

zucchini, in Basque-Style Sautéed Courgettes, 177